AF469063

Introducing drawing techniques

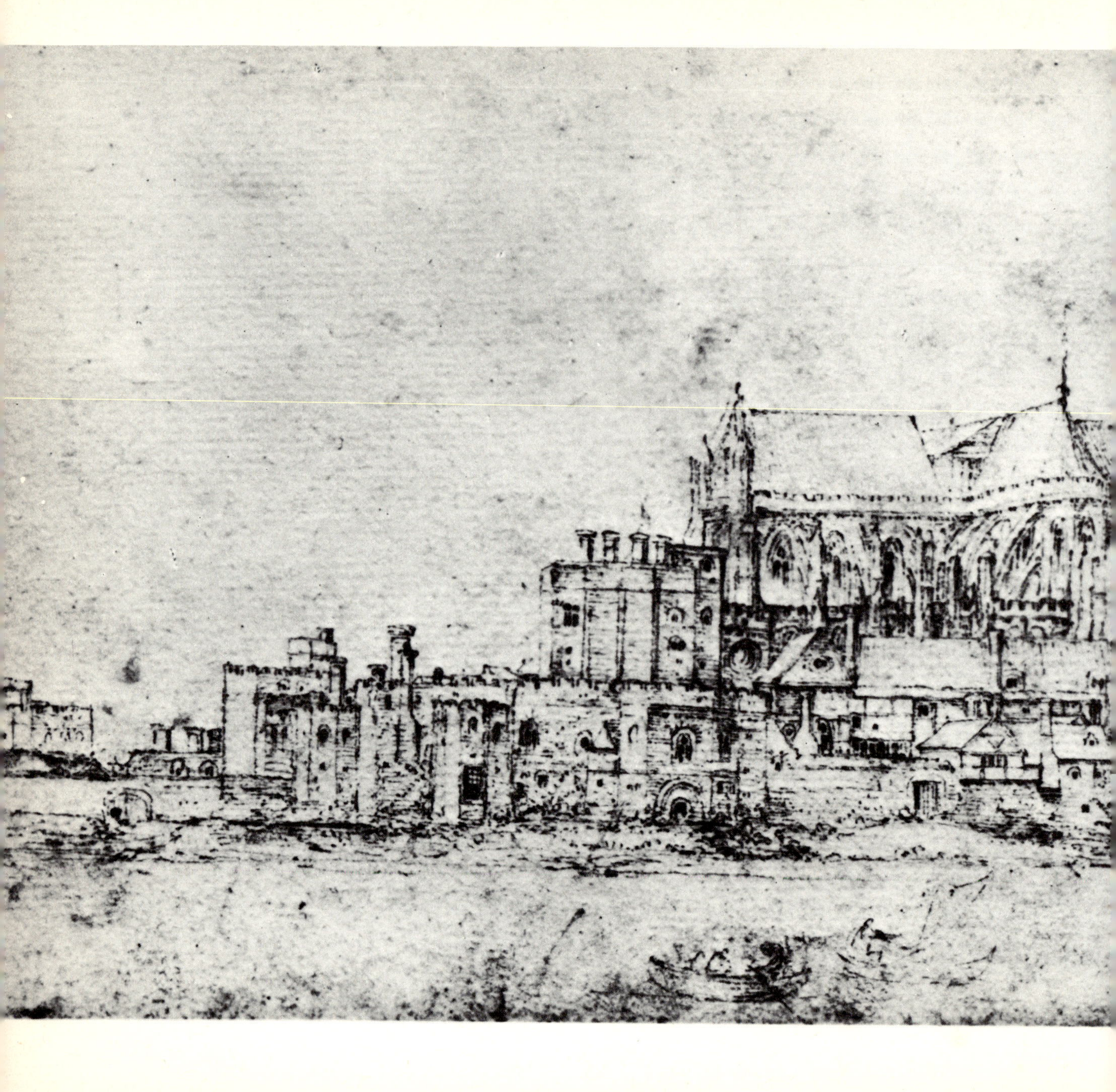

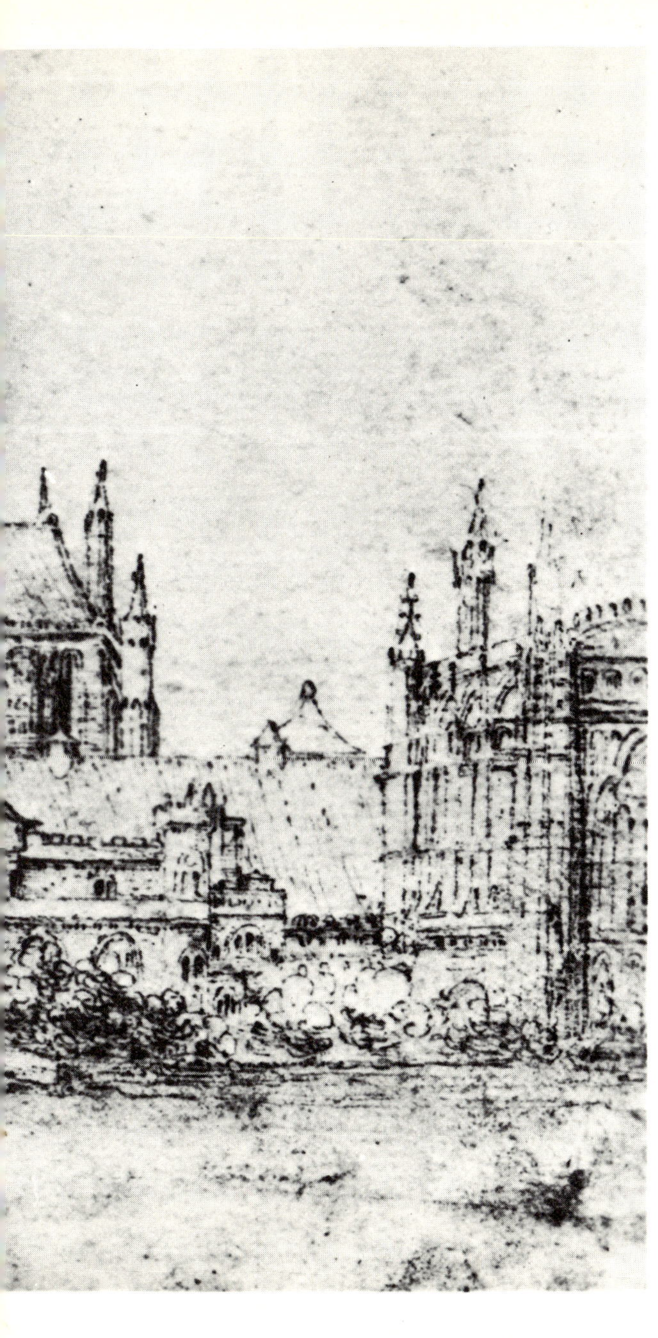

Introducing drawing techniques

Robin Capon

B T Batsford Limited
London

First published 1974
ISBN 0 7134 2444 3

Designed by Mark Gerlings, Libra Studios
Filmset in 11/12½ pt Monotype Bembo by
Servis Filmsetting Limited, Manchester
Printed and bound in Great Britain by
William Clowes and Sons Limited, Beccles, Suffolk
for the publishers
B T Batsford Limited
4 Fitzhardinge Street, London W1H 0AH

Title page
WENZEL HOLLAR: *Westminster Abbey and Parliament House from the Thames*
Pen and ink. Victoria and Albert Museum
Crown copyright

Contents

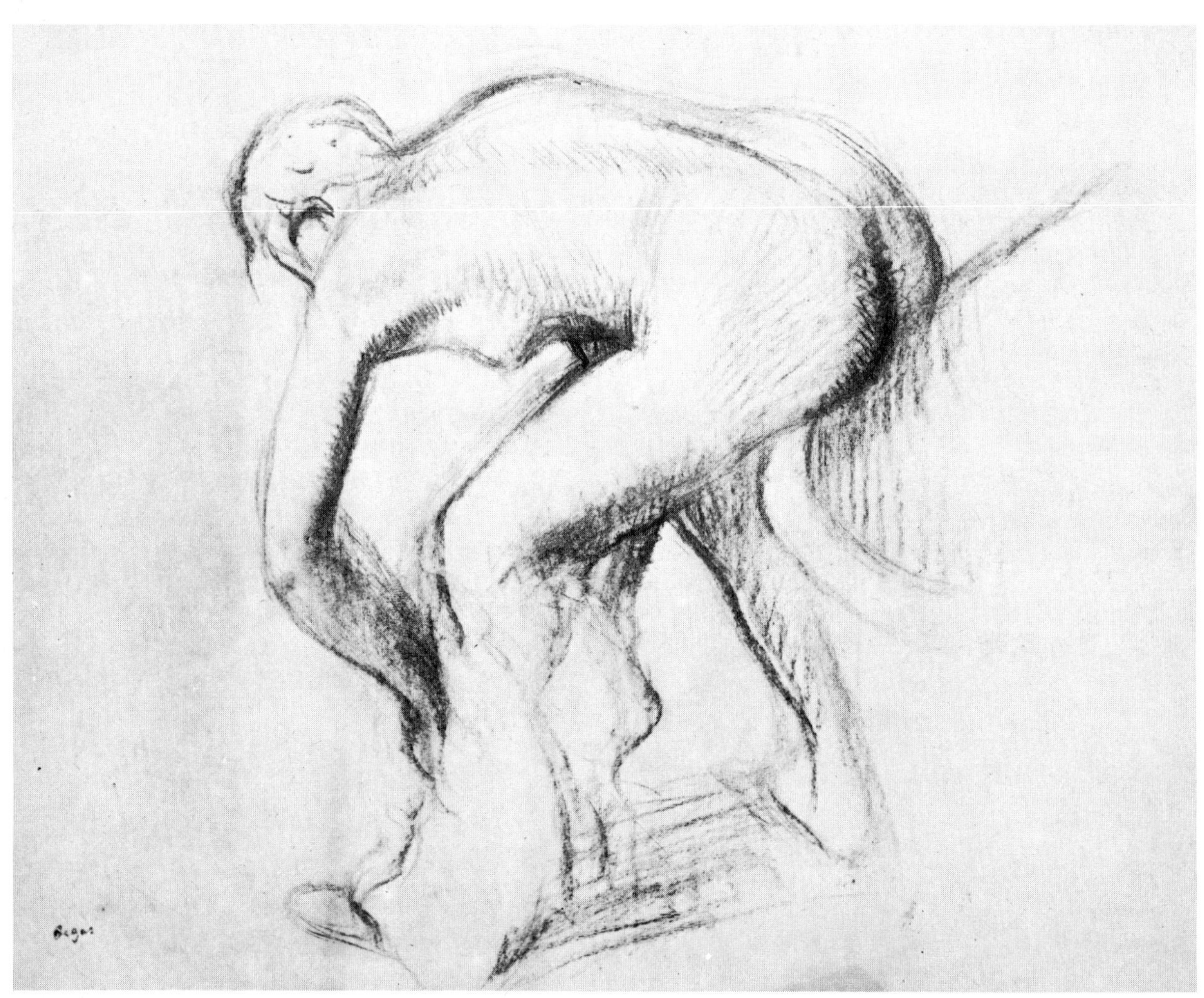

Introduction

My thanks are due to the Trustees of the following Galleries and Museums for providing photographs and allowing reproduction of drawings in their collections: the British Museum; the Tate Gallery; the Victoria and Albert Museum; the Ashmolean Museum, Oxford; the Royal Library, Windsor Castle.

I also thank Thelma M. Nye and Harriet Murray-Browne for their advice and help in the preparation of this book, and my wife, Patricia, for her hours of typing.

EDGAR DEGAS: *Nude drying herself*
Charcoal. Victoria and Albert Museum

Drawing is still regarded by some people simply as the act of representing objects on paper by the skilful use of pencil or pen. There are a few schools which still employ those who 'teach' drawing.

Drawing is an act of expression and only to a limited extent can it be taught. The expression may take an abstract or decorative form, or drawing may be used as the vehicle to convey ideas about particular objects, characters, scenes, etc. From cave art to that of Picasso, Matisse and Klee, drawing has been a vital part of art and a necessary part of life. The artist may choose from a variety of drawing implements and media, the choice depending as much on suitability of media to technique as on personal preferences.

Methods and techniques can be taught and learnt, for example, how to estimate proportions or plot perspective. One can be taught to be observant: formerly art was, to a large extent, based on the powers of the artist to observe and to set down his observations. Michelangelo is reputed to have said that ninety per cent of the work of the artist is taken up with thought and observation. What cannot be taught is how best to convey on paper one's thoughts or emotions. One cannot see through the eyes of someone else, neither can one experience their reactions. The artist may learn methods and techniques but his drawings are the result of his observations, his understanding, his imagination, his emotions and reactions. This may involve exaggeration or distortion of certain aspects of the subject whilst others are ignored.

Drawing is a basic and natural form of self expression; everyone can draw. Too often, however, students are timid, inhibited or suppressed; frequently they lack the knowledge of the many possible forms of drawing.

This book is written for people interested in drawing as a means of expression and creation. It is not a 'how to draw' book; its aim is to excite, to stimulate, and to describe and illustrate many drawing techniques and ideas. While using it, investigations could be made into how nature 'draws'; the ripples on water, for example, or the graphic expression of a naked tree against a dying winter sky. The way man has drawn across nature could also be considered—railway lines, motorways, pylons, cables, or the trails of smoke from jet planes, and so on. The work of well known artists should also be studied.

The illustrations and text combine to explain a particular technique or idea. The illustrations should not be regarded as the ultimate expression of that idea. The material in this book is intended as a starting point rather than something to be copied. Many of the ideas can lead to numerous variations and developments: far too many to attempt to illustrate within a single book.

Much of the equipment required is simple and inexpensive. Most homes, schools, or studios will already have many of the drawing instruments and materials suggested.

Line

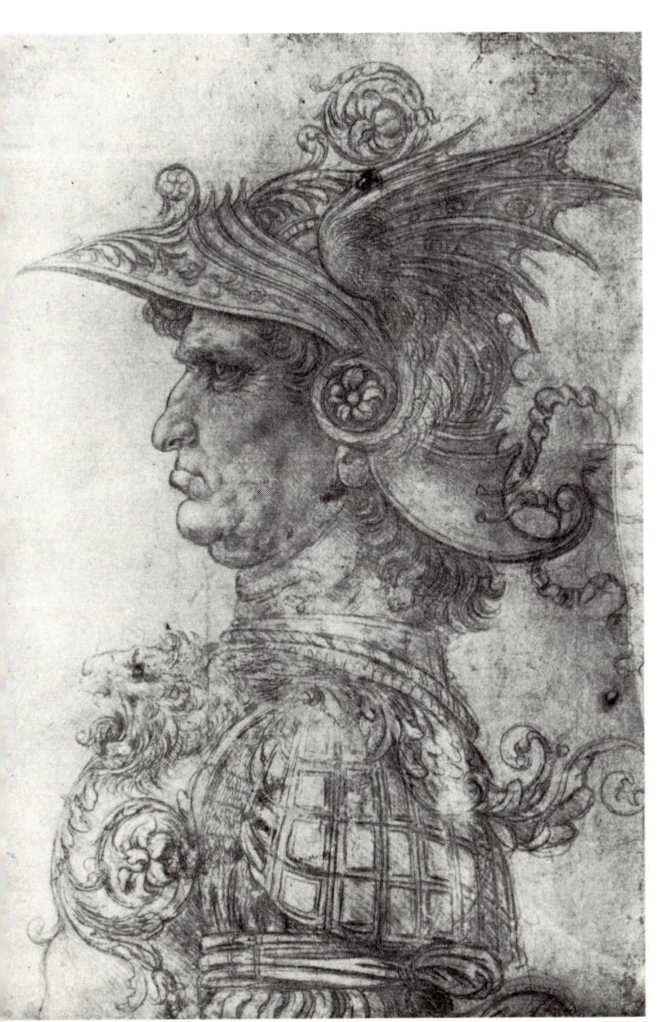

The hunters of early civilizations scratched images of animals on the walls of their caves. These were probably the first examples of graphic art and the choice of subject matter was very significant. The lives of these peoples depended on their success at trapping and killing these wild beasts. The drawings were often linear in concept, engraved with a flint into the bare rock surface.

Man has always instinctively been an artist and has wished to record, whether on a rock surface or paper or canvas, those things which have seemed important and worth expressing. A young child early on makes marks with a crayon and soon begins to build up a graphic vocabulary in this way. Drawing is a necessary and important means of self-expression.

The drawings of most young children are confident; a personal language, often charged with details not immediately obvious to the casual observer. The wise adult will foster and encourage this mode of expression. But in an age of mass media

LEONARDO DA VINCI: *Warrior*
Silverpoint. The British Museum

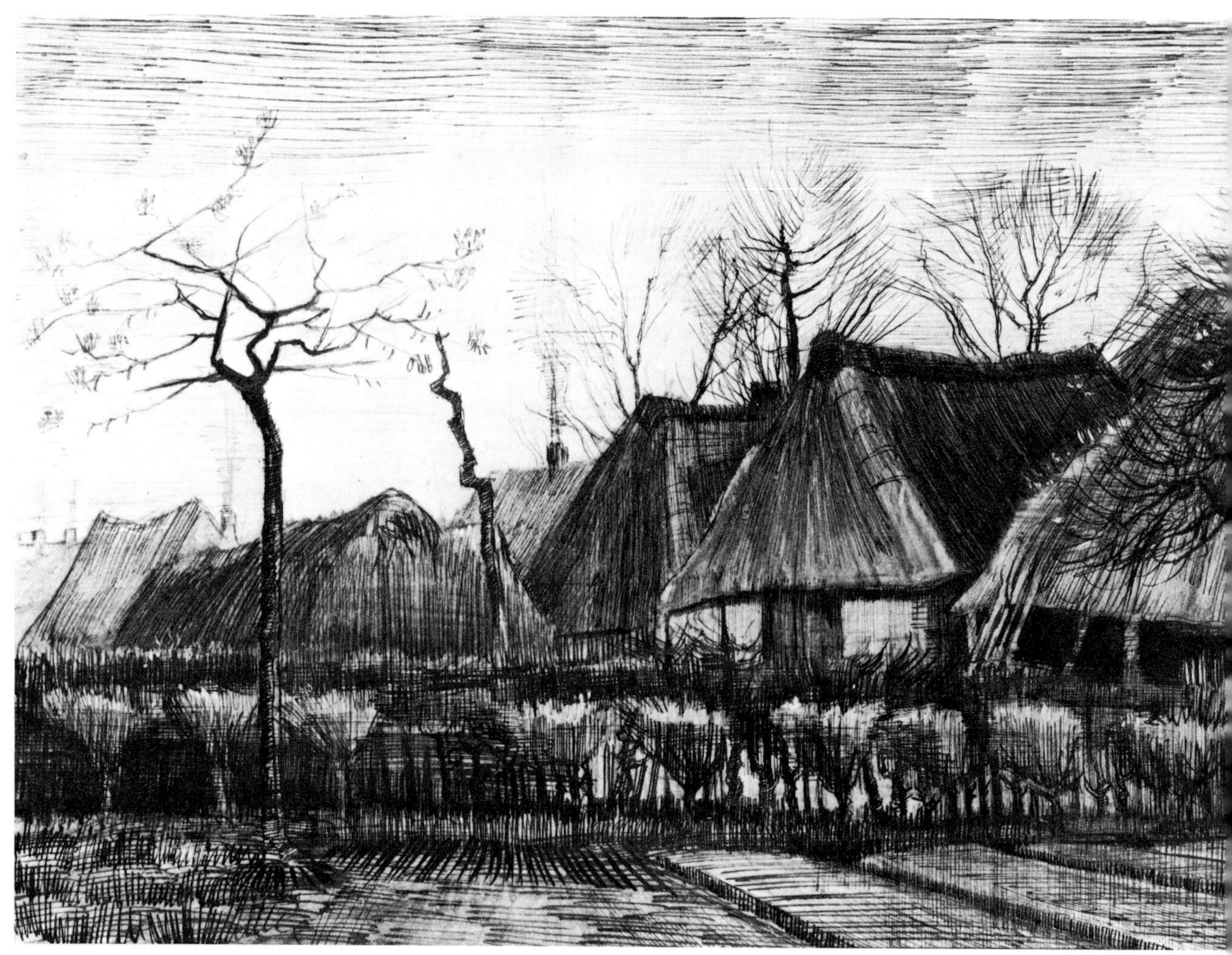

VINCENT VAN GOGH: *Thatched Roofs*
Pen drawing. The Tate Gallery, London

and pressures and influences from the outside world, children often lose confidence and interest in their own efforts, particularly during adolescence.

It may be necessary at this stage to restore confidence and rekindle interest and this is the aim of the first section of this book. Figures 1 to 70 show a development from simple marks and scribbles to sophisticated linear drawings. These examples are not meant as a step-by-step guide to perfect draughtsmanship, but it is hoped that they will stimulate interest and enthusiasm for drawing as well as showing various techniques and possible avenues for exploration. Naturally, different techniques and ideas will suit different people. Confident drawing, although relying to an extent on knowledge and experience, is also based on practice and perseverance.

It is as well to bear in mind that drawing is not simply confined to the use of pencil or pen. If one cuts into a sheet of paper with a pair of scissors, one is in effect drawing, likewise a design may be scratched into soft metal with a sharp point. Exciting designs can be made with a finger dipped in paint or ink, a stick, a comb, a piece of card and so on. It should be remembered that each idea or technique is open to various developments by employing different drawing tools. Experiments with various papers and supports may also give interesting results.

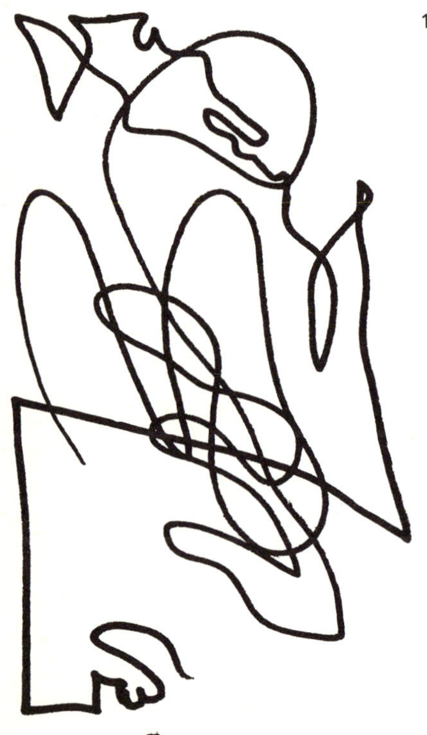

1

2

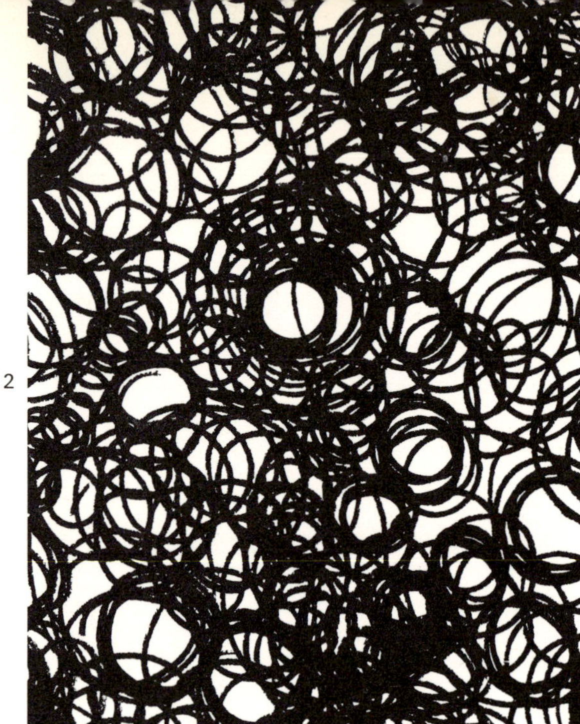

3

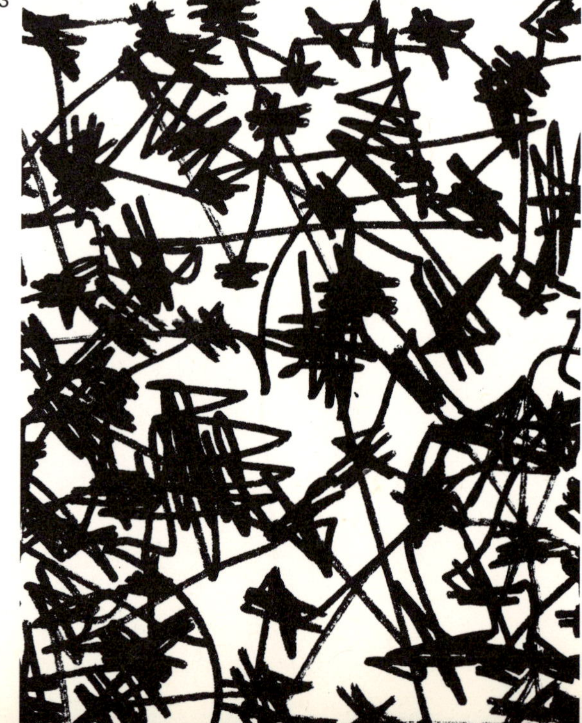

Scribble

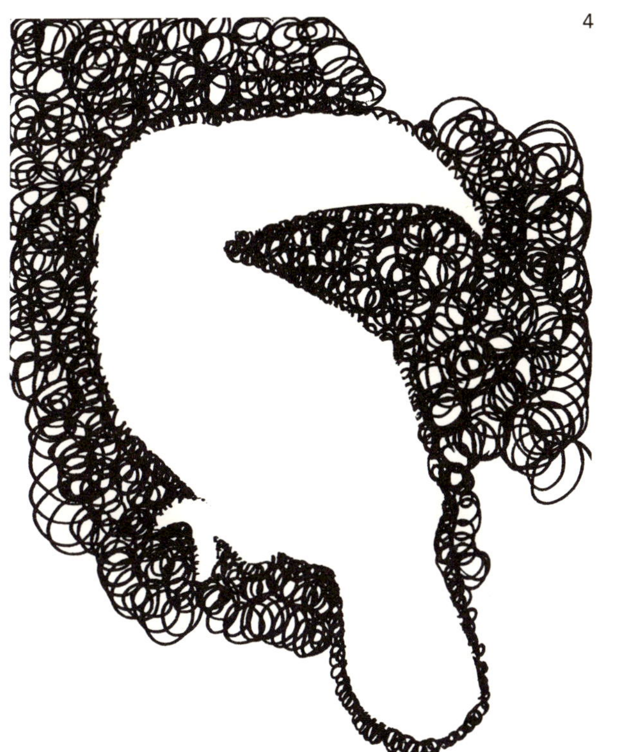

4

An early stage in the development of the drawing of young children is the use of scribble. Besides being a new found technique, it is an important progression in co-ordination and rhythm. Some artists have used the technique as a starting point for more complex design work; it is said that Leonardo da Vinci was sometimes inspired by blot or scribble drawings.

Scribbling may serve a number of useful purposes. It can be used to purge inhibitions and regain confidence with a particular drawing implement or medium; it can suggest forms and ideas for further development; or it may be employed to create a rhythmic design or texture.

Figures 1 to 4 are scribble drawings. In figure 2 scribbling has been used to effect an interesting abstract design. Variations in size and intensity have been employed. Figure 3 shows the use of 'continuous' scribble, and in figure 4 it has been used to make up the background of a silhouetted shape.

Continuous line

Drawing with a continuous line offers various possibilities. Again, it is a technique which can be used for pure experiment or to suggest ideas for further expansion and development. On the other hand, shapes formed by allowing a single line to overlap on itself might form the basic design of a painting. Employing this technique for a representational-type drawing often leads to a test of imagination and ingenuity.

Often the restriction of 'rules' or disciplines in the creation of a work of art can add to its unity and interest. The 'rule' with continuous line drawing is that the drawing implement should not be removed from the paper until the drawing is complete, although it is possible to travel back along lines already drawn. This has happened in figure 5.

In figure 6 the line has been allowed to overlap on itself to produce different shapes and intensities. Many variations are possible. Many kinds of media may be used and on a much larger scale.

Interesting experiments with a continuous line may result from drawing with the left hand; drawing with eyes closed; drawing with a foot; or by drawing with both hands simultaneously.

5

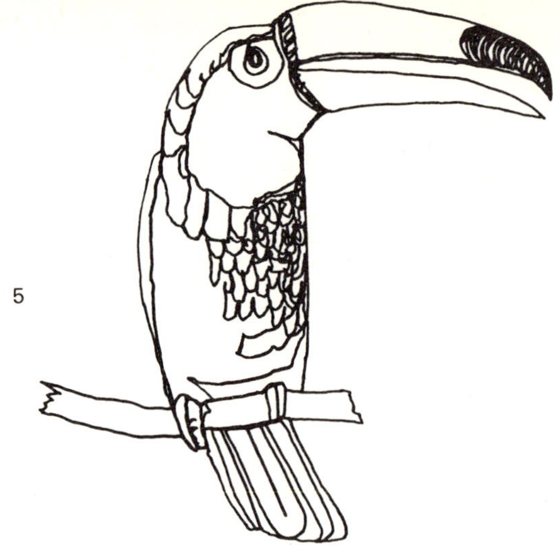

6

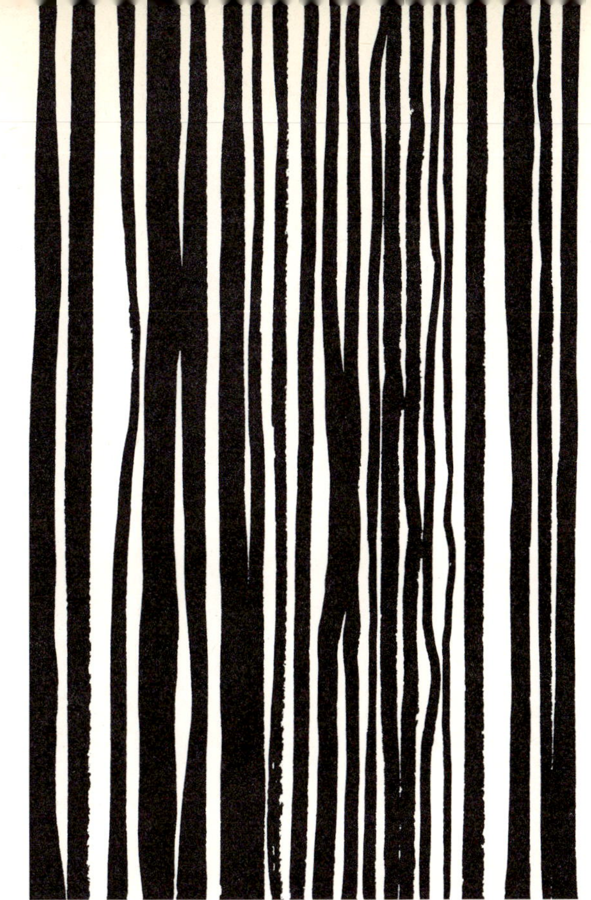

7

Straight line

Straight lines may be drawn freehand or with the aid of a ruler or some other form of straight-edge. The lines may vary in thickness, in length, or in direction. Different media may be used, perhaps to compose a single drawing.

Figure 7 is made up of straight lines drawn with a brush, using a ruler. The spacing is unequal, and lines of different thickness have been obtained by varying the amount of pressure applied to the brush.

Figure 8 is a drawing with a ball-point pen, employing different lengths and directions.

Figure 9 shows a combination of all four qualities to make a representational drawing of houses.

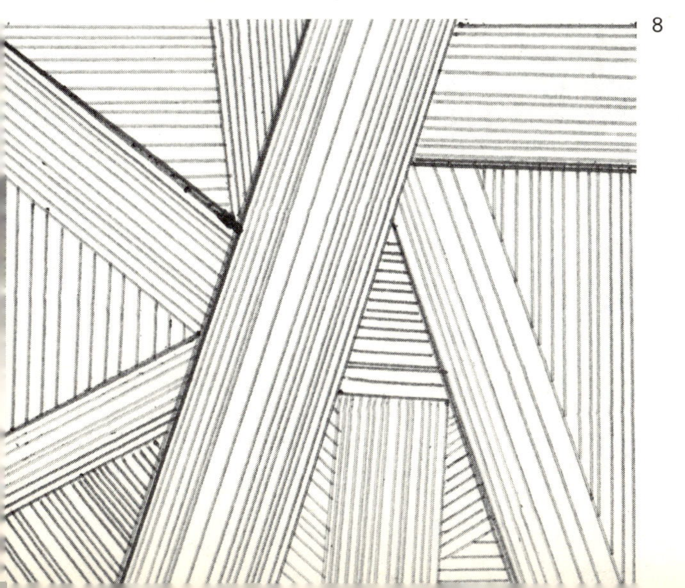

8

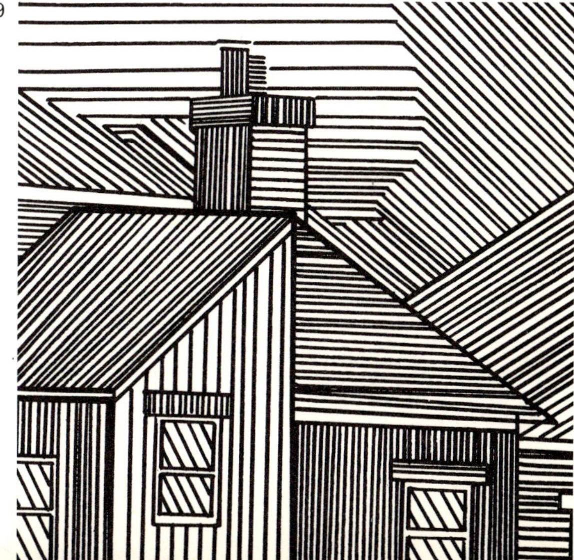

9

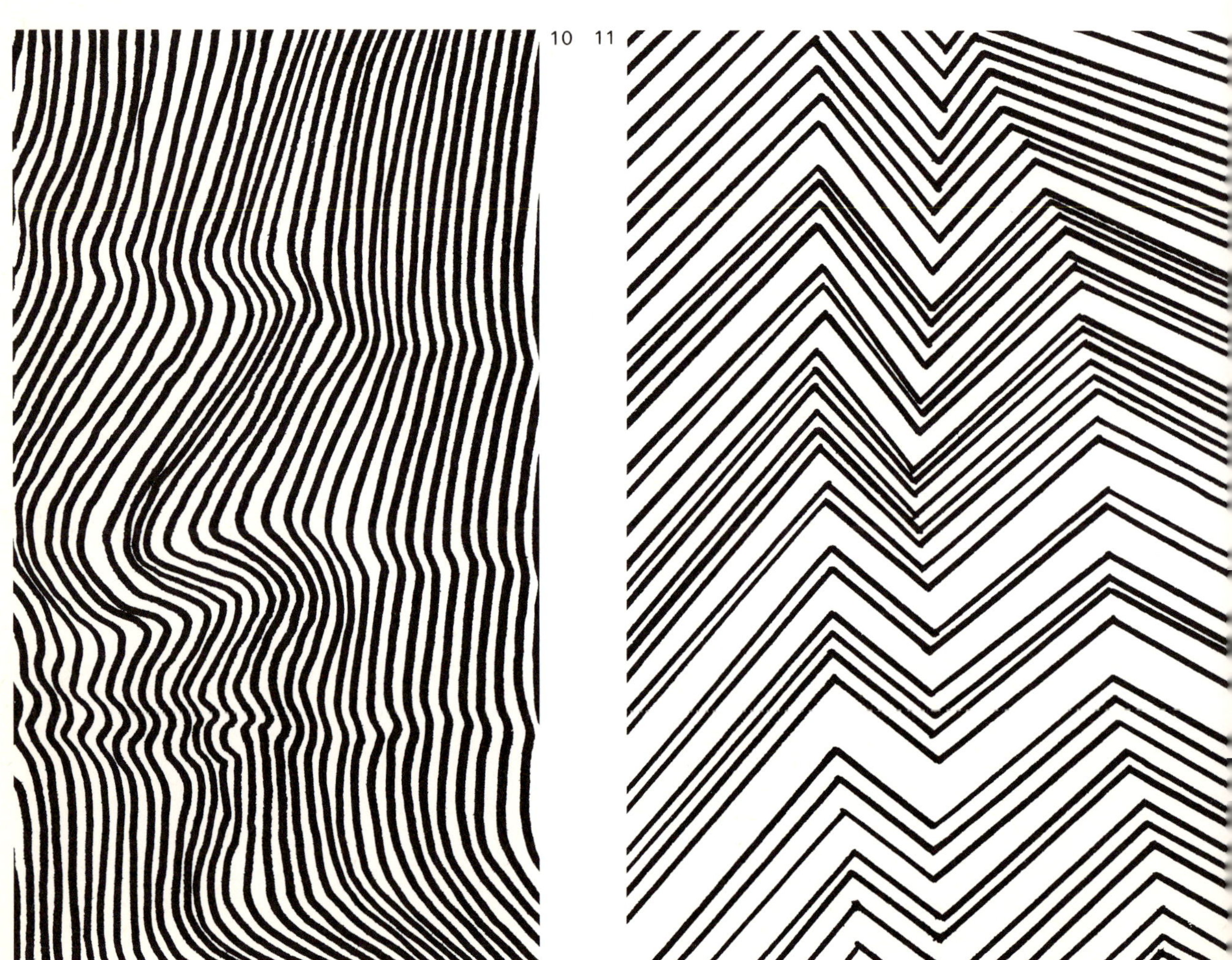

10 11

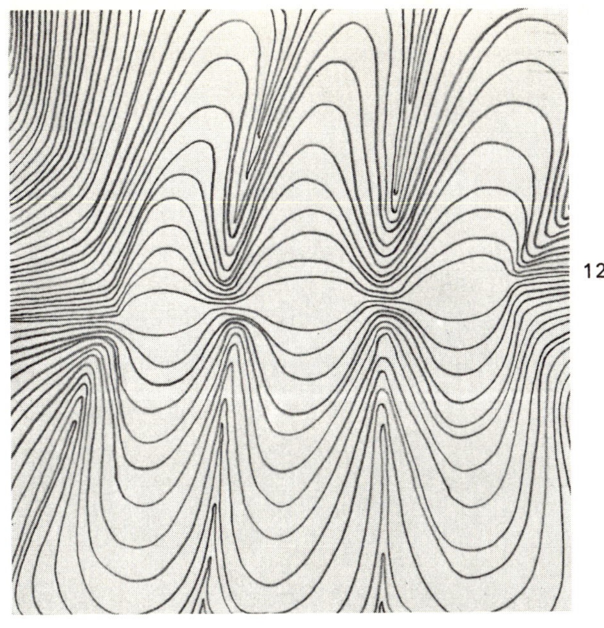

12

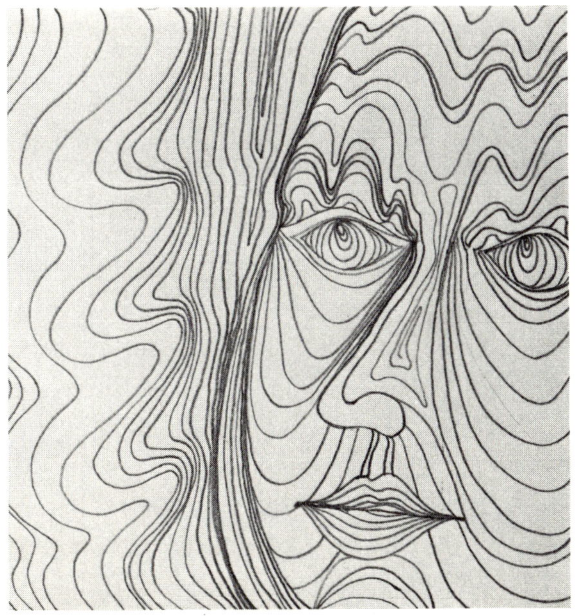

13

Wavy line

Wavy lines are best drawn freehand. Designs of this type are useful as exercises to encourage confidence in drawing, but they can be used to make interesting linear drawings in their own right, see figure 13. Again, one can make use of variations in thickness, spacing and 'flow'.

Repetition of a single wavy line, drawn freehand and spaced evenly, can give powerful optical effects, see figure 10. In figure 11 a ruler was used, the line being repeated at different intervals. Figure 12 shows the expansion of wavy lines from the centre of the paper, varying the spacing to create areas of greater intensity.

14 15

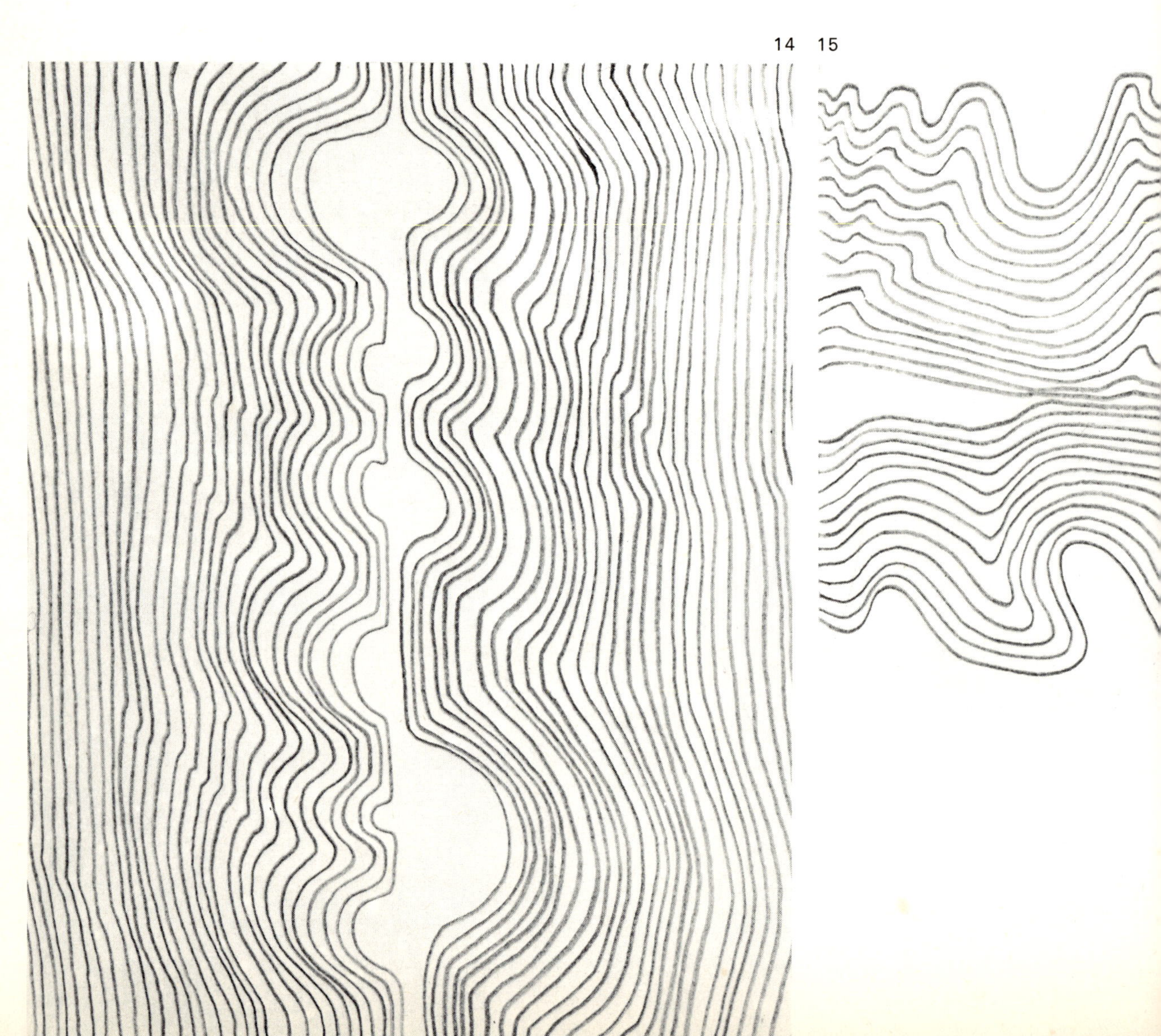

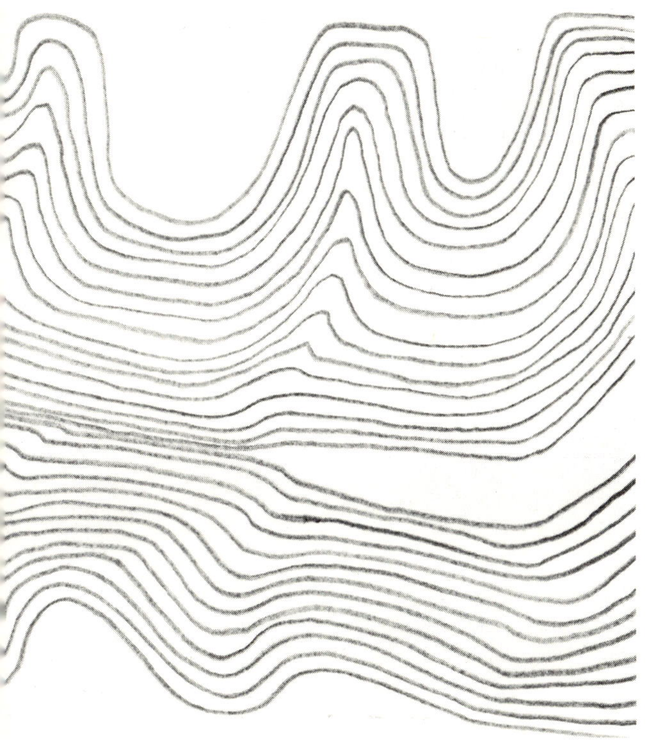

Designing from the centre

Designs which are based on the repetition of lines either side of the centre, as in figure 12, can be effective. The repetition of a line with a number of kinks is often enough in itself to produce an interesting drawing. When the line is being reproduced it should be followed as accurately as possible, the same distance being maintained. Lines repeated in this way tend gradually to even out.

Lines may be repeated from the centre outwards as in figure 14; from the edges inwards, figure 15; from diagonals, or from other areas of the paper.

These drawings are best kept to a small scale; the ones illustrated were made with pencil.

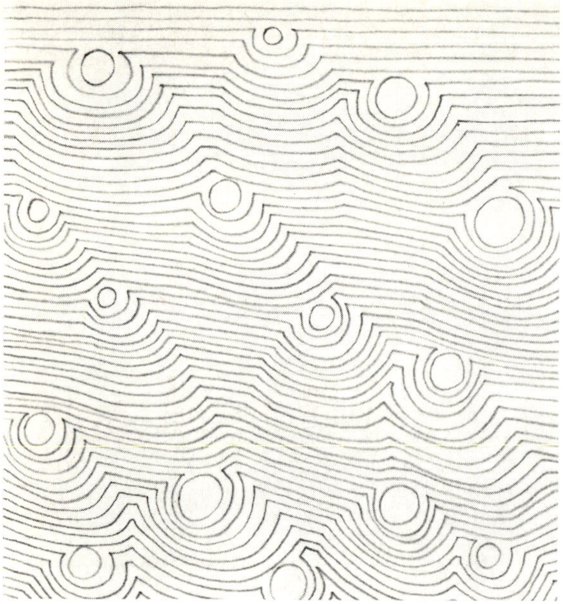

16

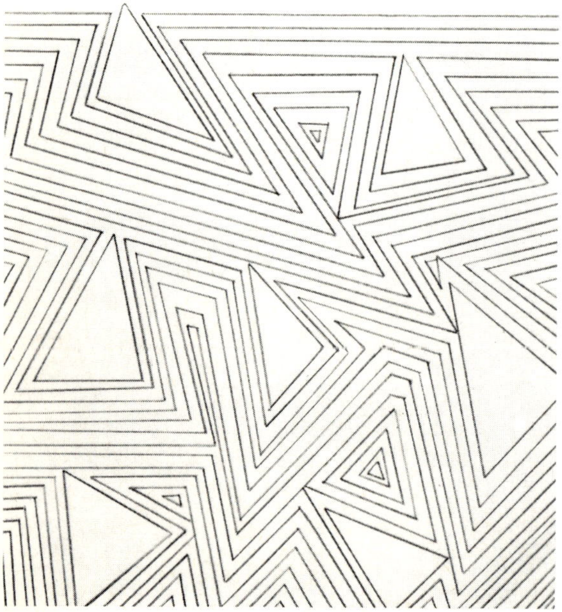

17

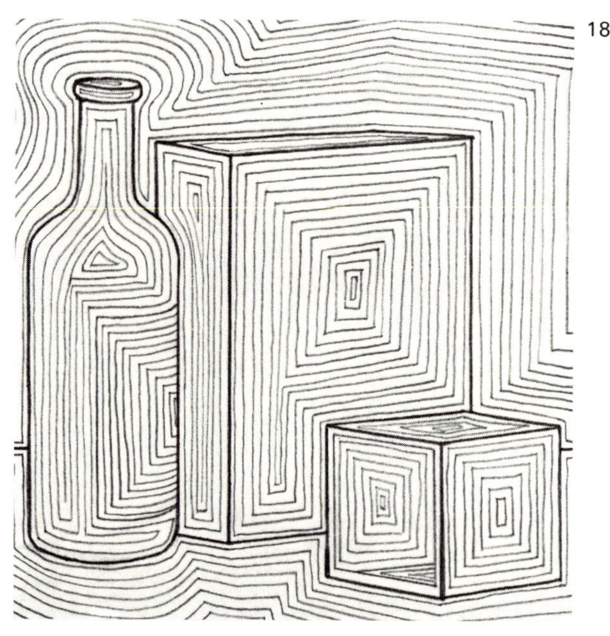

18

19

Interrupted line

The 'rule' here is that lines are drawn across the paper but should they meet a shape, they are made to follow round it before continuing. The lines may be drawn freehand, as in figures 16, 18 and 19, or with the aid of a straight-edge, as in figure 17. They may cross the paper vertically, horizontally or diagonally.

Figures 16, 17 and 19 show how different 'obstacles' are used to interrupt linear flow.

In figure 18 a still-life group has been made up of lines following particular shapes.

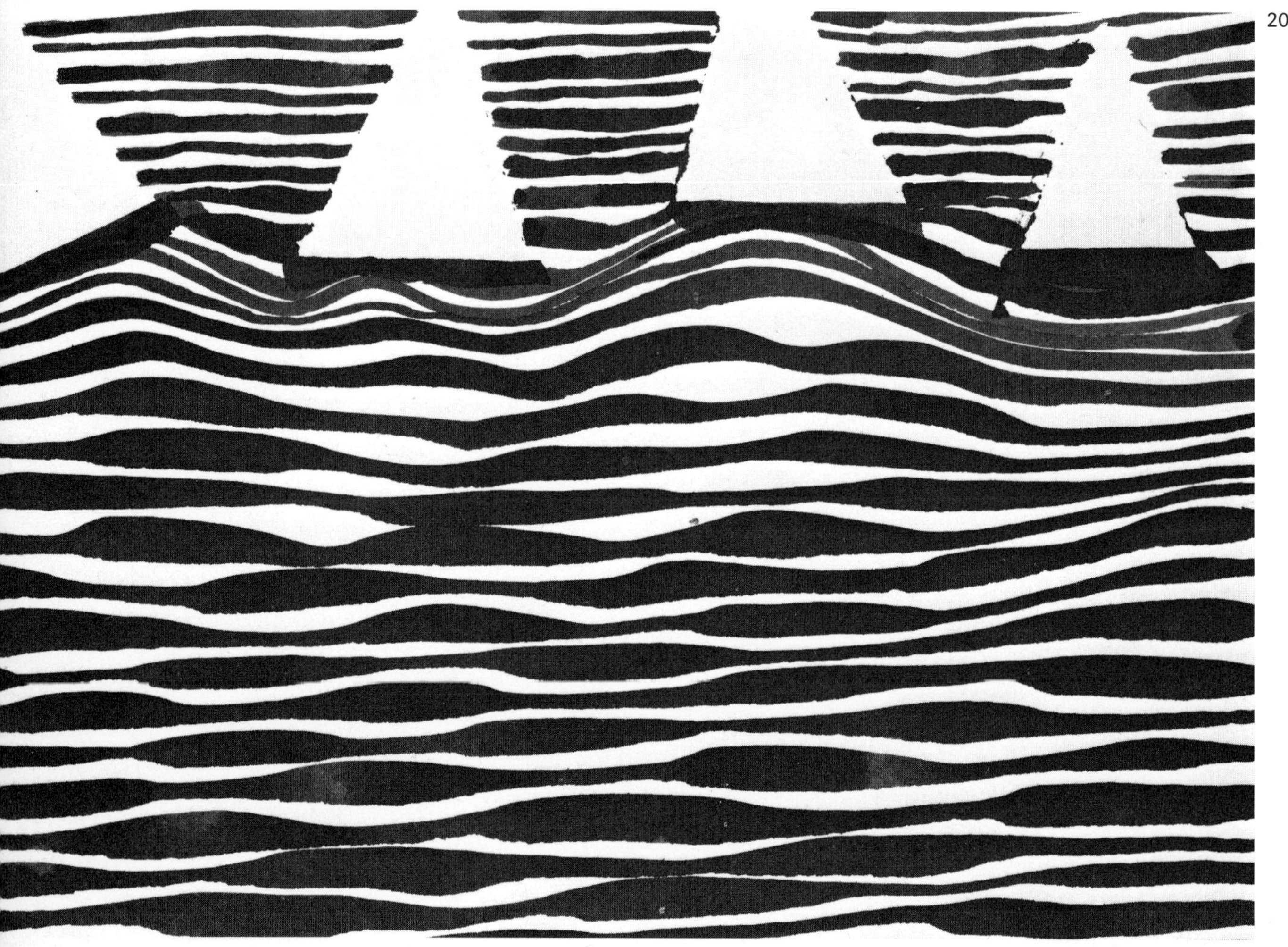

20

Rhythmic line

21

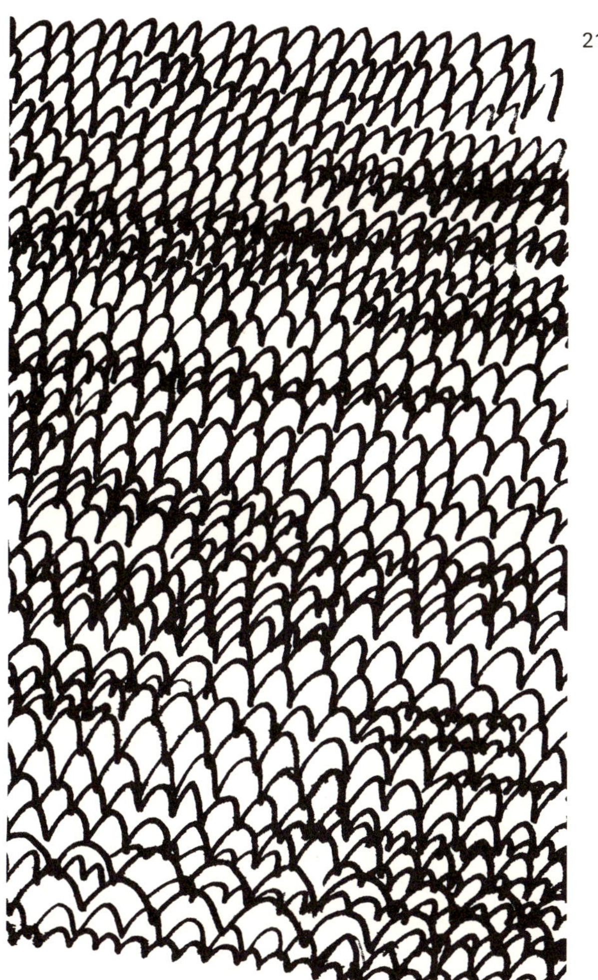

A line may be repeated in a definite rhythm or employ a rhythmic movement of the hand in its making. Flowing lines made in this way may suggest obvious pictures, as in figure 20, or might simply be used to create texture, decorative or pattern effects.

Figure 21: flowing lines overlapped in parts to create areas of differing intensity. Handwriting patterns produce similar effects.

Figure 22 shows variations of pressure applied to an ink-laden brush.

22

Wet paper and resist techniques

Lines made on wet paper with a pen or brush blur and divide into delicate patterns, see figure 23. Lines drawn with a brush on paper which has just been heavily coated with fixative will produce the effect illustrated in figure 24. Ink and turpentine or ink and wax will produce similar resist properties.

23

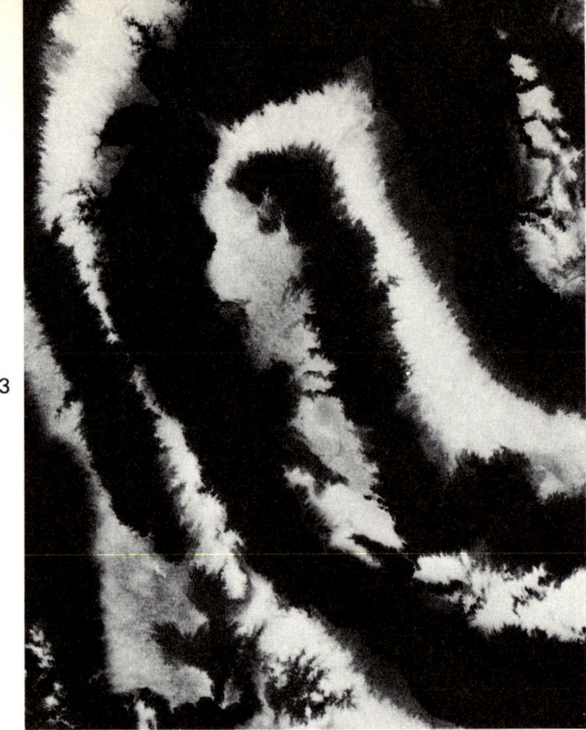

24

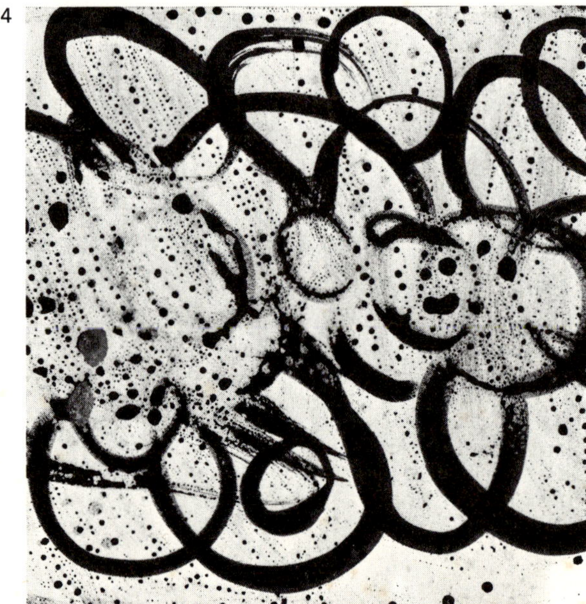

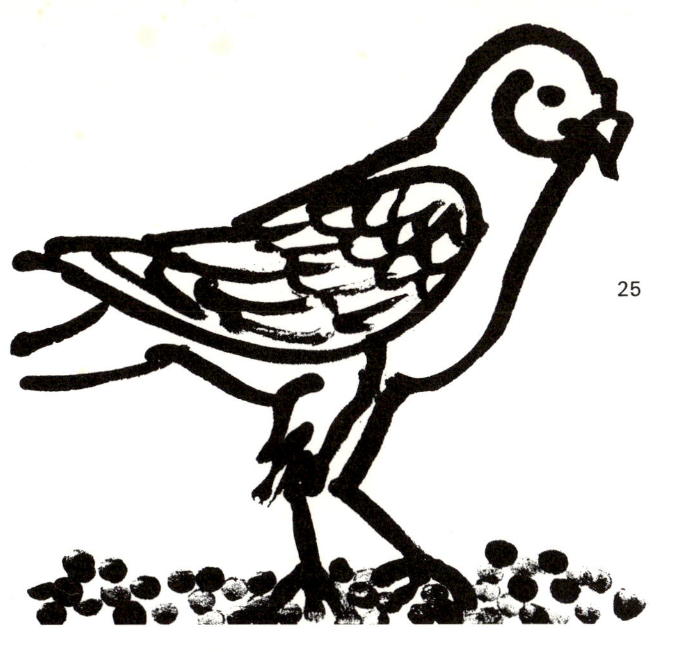

25

Finger drawing

As the name implies, the drawing is done with a finger, usually the first, dipped in ink or paint. Lines and dots can be made in this way, and several colours may be used. Similarly, shallow relief designs can be made by drawing into wet plaster or clay. See figures 25 and 26.

26

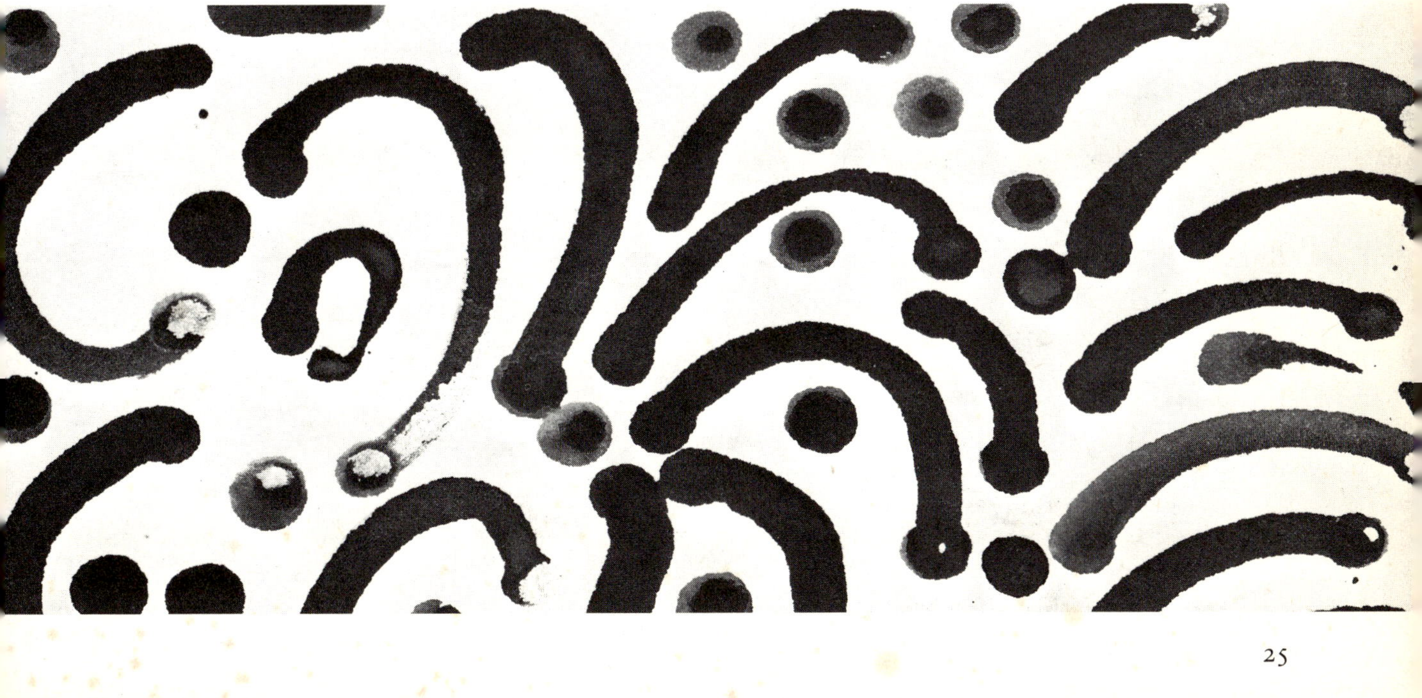

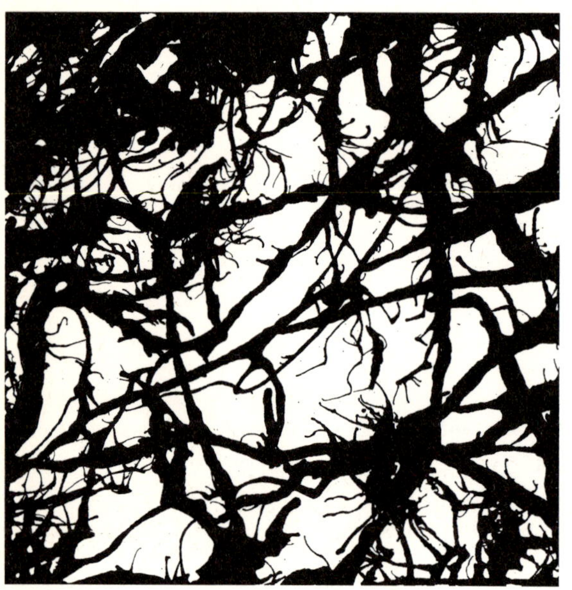

27

Blown line

Drops of paint or ink may be blown into lines, either directly, or through a drinking straw. The paint or ink must be of a fluid consistency. Designs may be made up by superimposing blown lines of different colours. Each colour should be allowed to dry if a clear definition is required, though the ramification of different colours may produce interesting results.

Figure 27 shows lines blown inwards from the edges.

Figure 28 is a drawing of a fish made by blown lines with added brushwork.

Linear drawings can also be made from 'runs' of paint or ink. The lines are made by allowing drops of paint or ink to run across the paper by tilting it at various angles. To a certain extent the direction of the line can be controlled by altering the tilt of the paper. Lines being made in this way tend to merge with existing lines if still wet. It may be necessary, therefore, to allow the design to dry if lines are to be superimposed.

Figure 29 is a simple linear design made from 'runs'. In figure 30 the original lines have been crossed by others to form shapes, some of which have been shaded in.

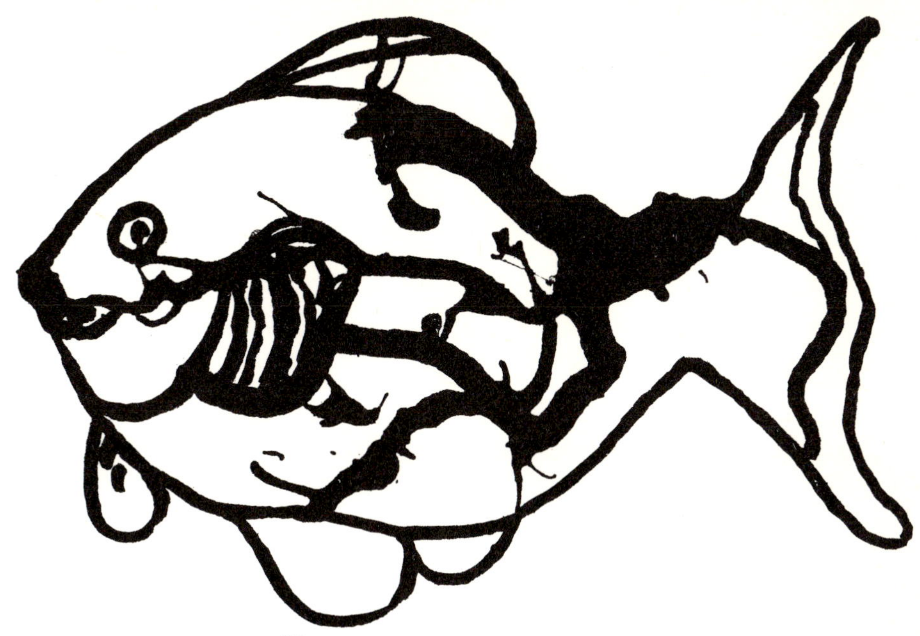

28

29 30

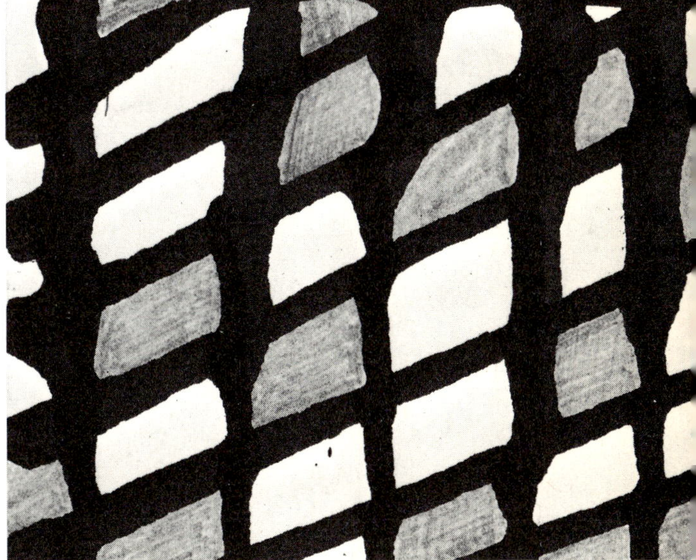

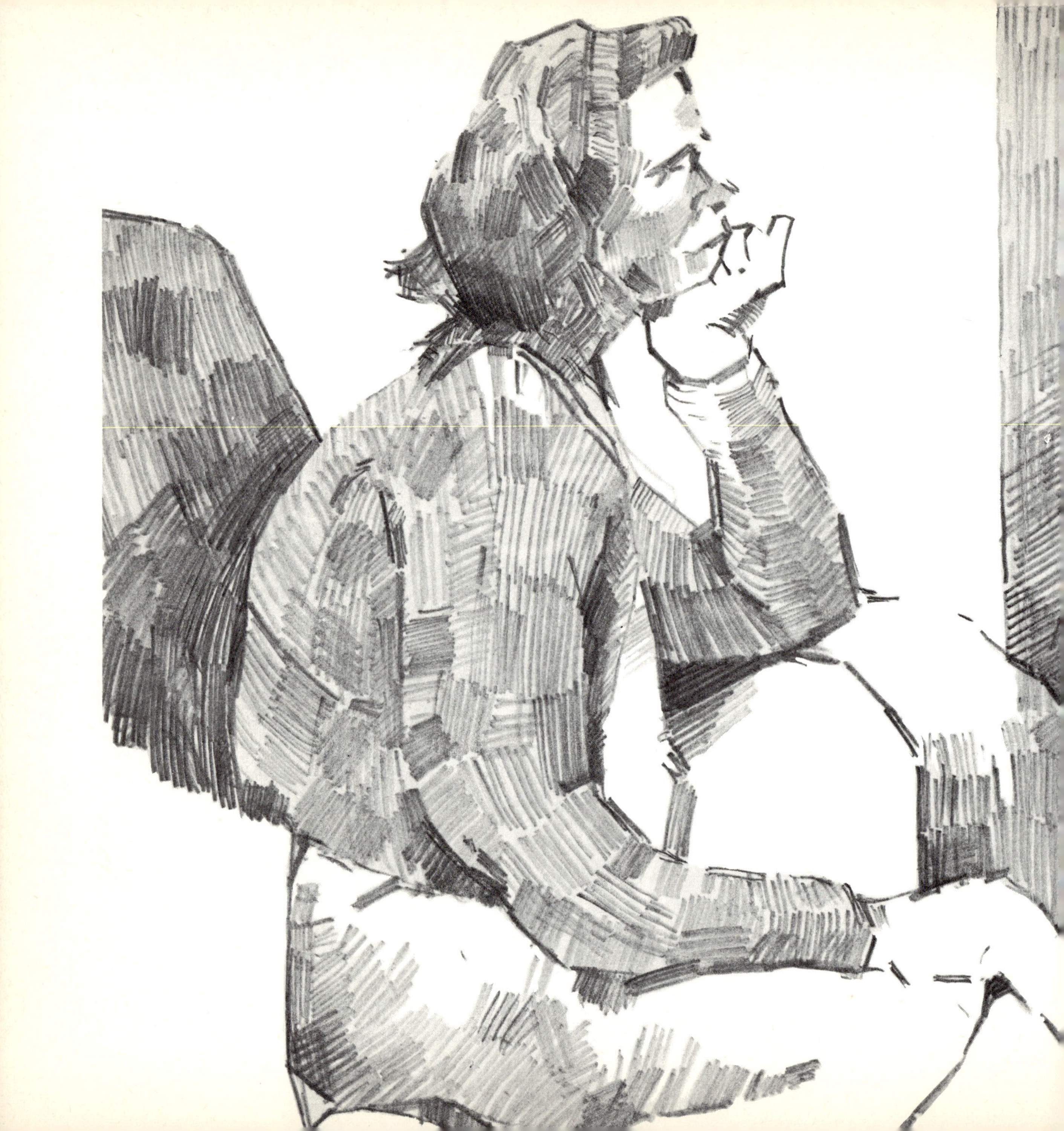

Hatched line

31 Rows or patches of short strokes can be used to build up a form or an abstract design. Variations may be achieved in tone (by pressure), thickness, spacing, direction and intensity.

Figures 31 and 32 illustrate two very different designs using a hatching technique.

Alternatively the hatched line can be allowed to flow, as in figure 33.

Incidentally, each of these three illustrations employs a different medium: figure 31 pencil, figure 32 ink, and figure 33 charcoal pencil. The student of drawing should be encouraged to experiment with different media, even within the confines of a single technique.

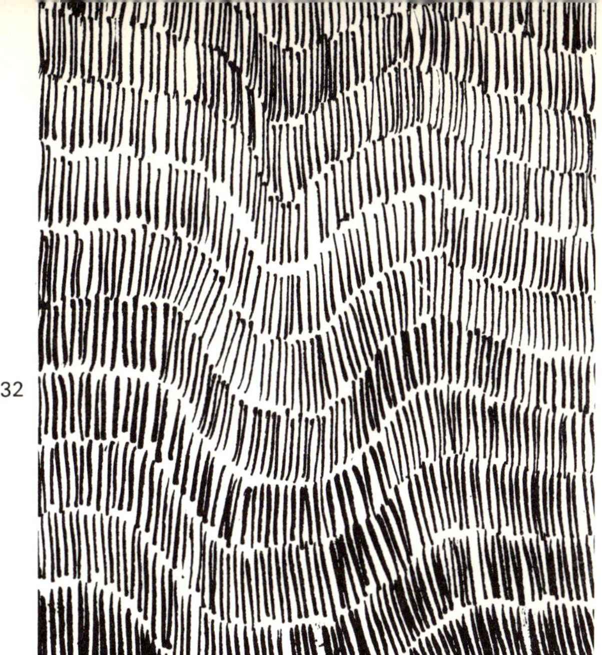

32

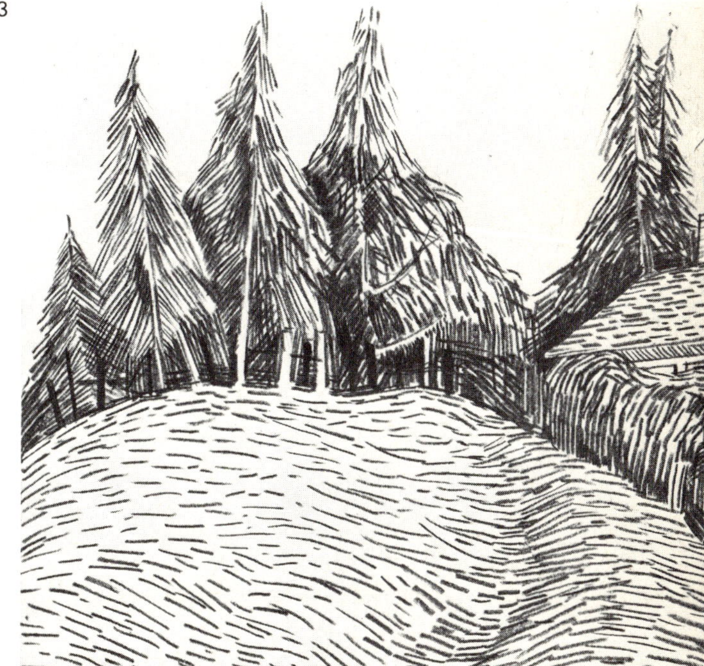

33

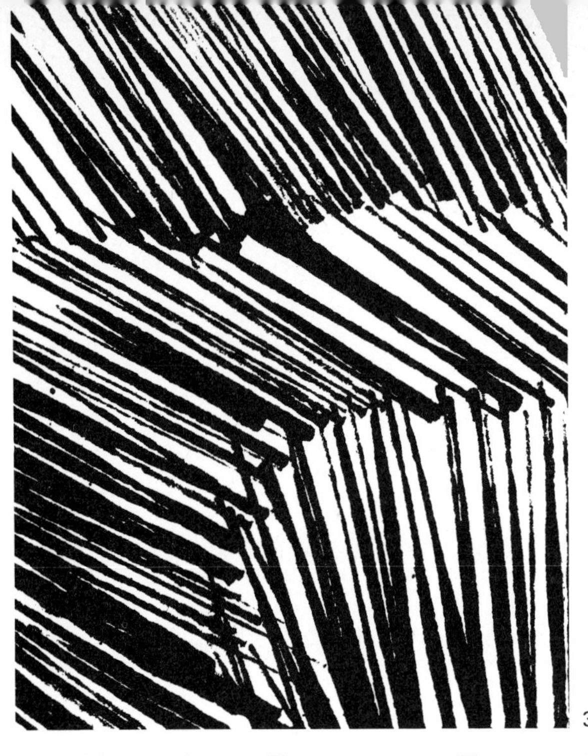

34

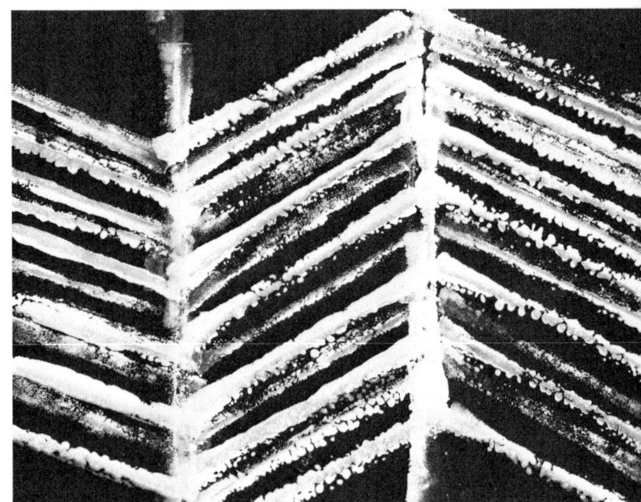

36

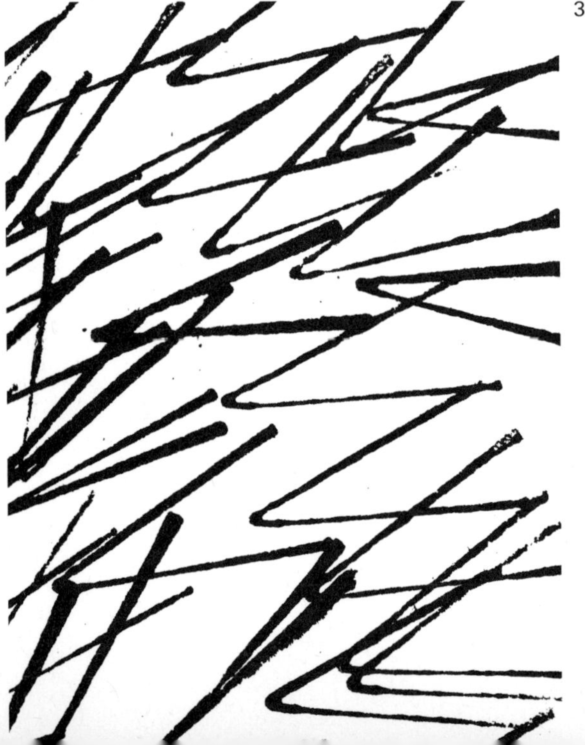

35

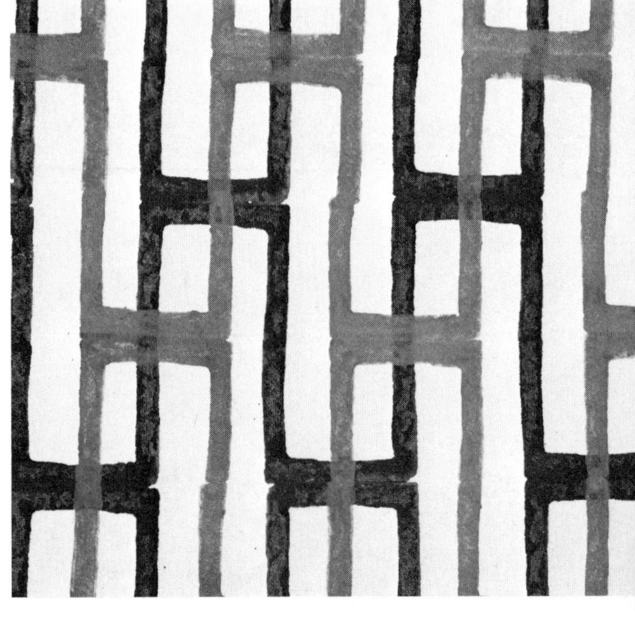

37

Offset line

Lines may be offset in a number of ways. Figures 34 and 35 illustrate the use of small lengths of card dipped in paint to build up a design. As before, the paint must be reasonably fluid. In figure 34 a single length of card has been offset in various directions, whilst in figure 35 a bent piece of card has produced a 'v' shape.

Lines may be offset in other ways, as with a roller in figure 36, from a cut potato shape in figure 37, and with a comb in figure 38.

Figure 39 shows a drawing of a hen made up entirely by offsetting from a single length of card.

38

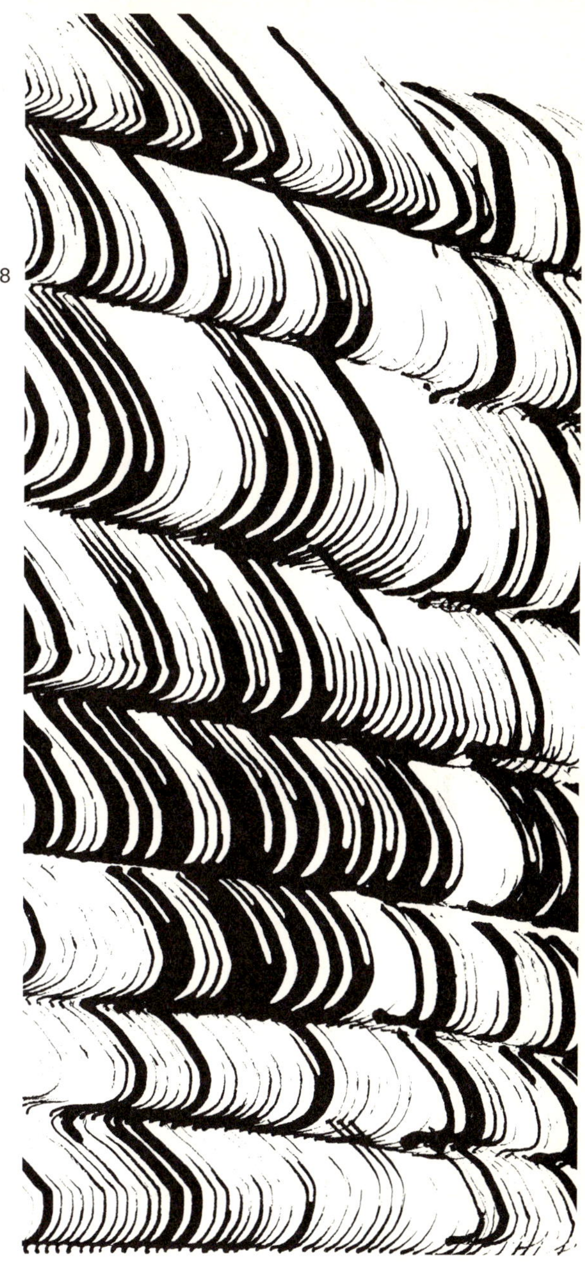

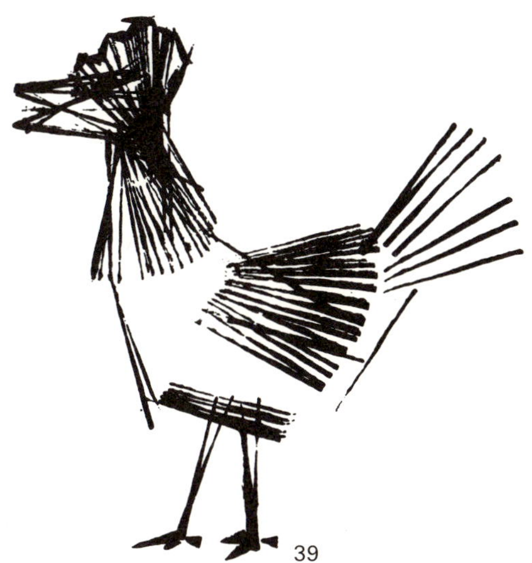

39

Blot drawing

Blot designs are best made on cartridge (drawing) paper, which is reasonably absorbent, using a quick-drying paint, such as poster colour, or indian ink. One piece of paper can be folded or two separate sheets used. In figure 40 the drawing was made with ink and brush on the right-hand half of the paper, and transferred to the left-hand half by folding and pressing down. The drawing was done in stages, working from the top downwards, and each stage was transferred before continuing with the next. Some pencil drawing was added at the base.

Charcoal can be offset in a similar way, as in figure 41, which has a superimposed ink design. Charcoal, as with other media, may need a certain amount of touching up on the left-hand side.

41

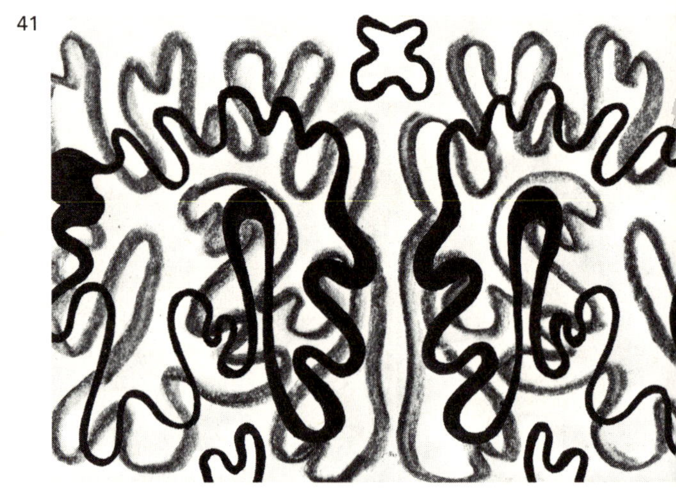

40

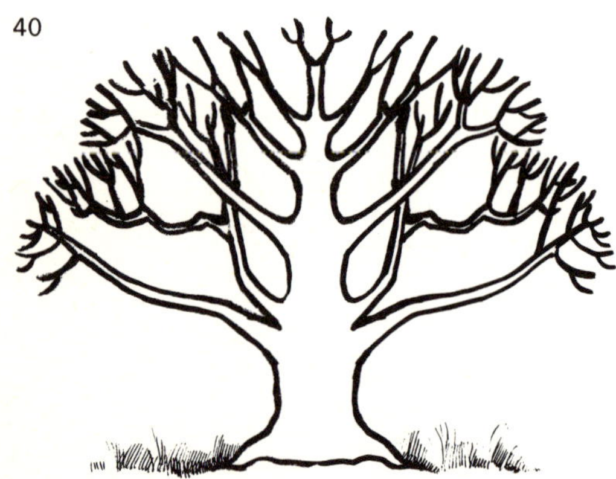

42

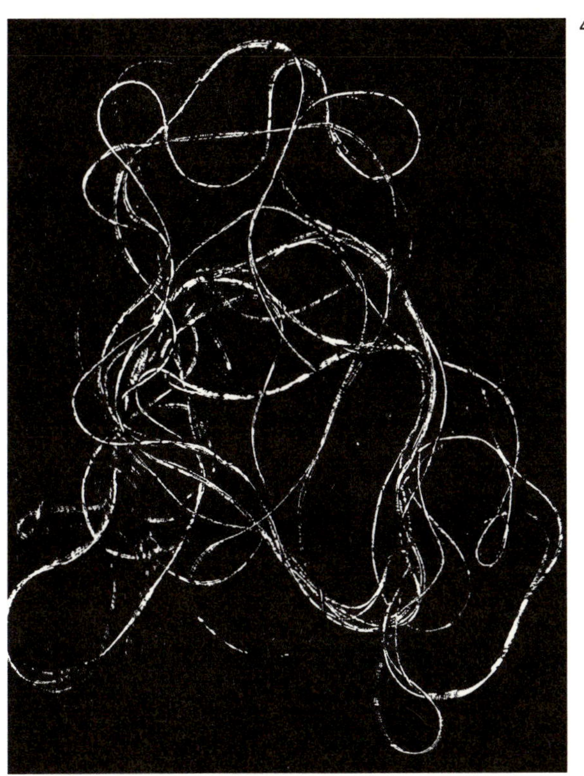

Print impressions

Impressions made by employing various simple printmaking techniques can produce interesting linear results. It is not the place of this book to detail these, but interesting experiments can be made with various drawing and masking techniques, using a bed of printing ink. Other books on this particular subject will provide many ideas for those who wish to explore this kind of work in depth, and some suggestions for further reading are made in the bibliography at the end of the book.

Figure 42 is an impression or print from a length of string which has been rolled with printing ink.

In figures 43 and 44 string was used to mask out lines on a bed of ink. Figure 44 shows a print of this with the string in position on the inked base, and figure 43 shows what happens when the string is removed.

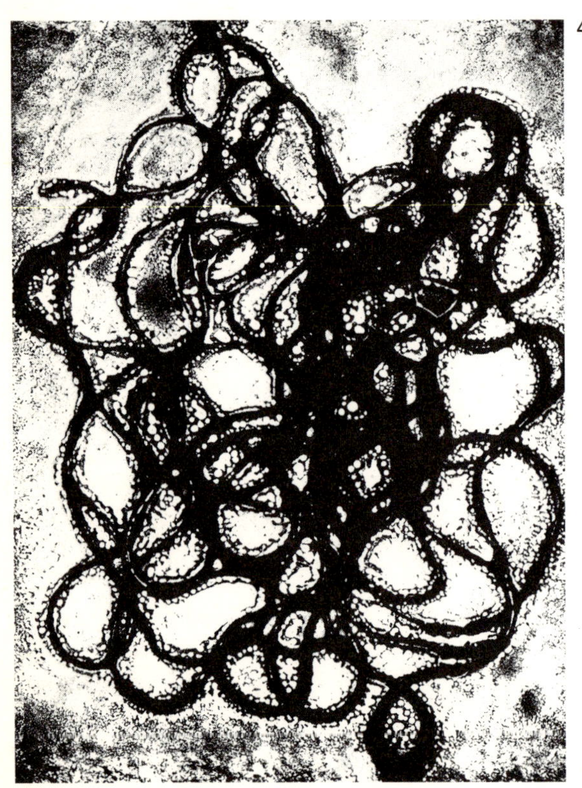

43

44

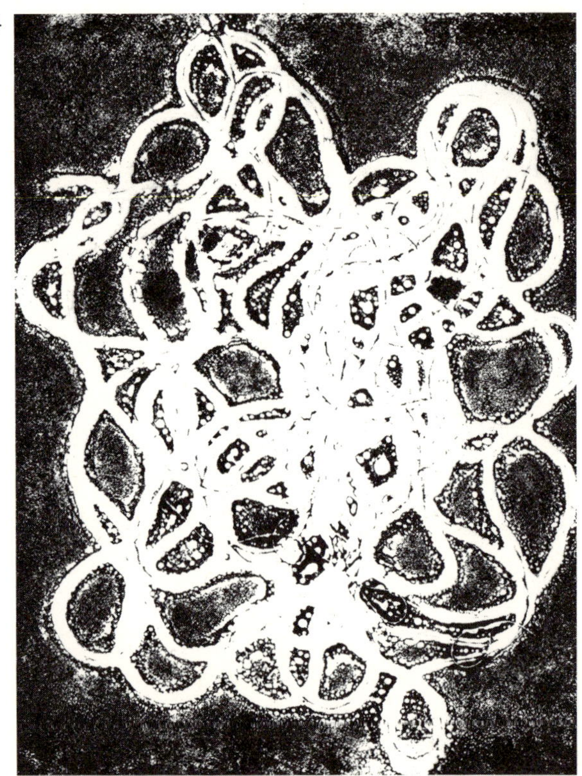

Impressed pencil designs

Figure 45 is an impressed pencil drawing. The paper is folded in half and the design drawn on one of the outer sides, pressing down heavily so as to create an impression on the paper beneath. The paper is then opened out and shaded over with a short stick of Conté crayon used on its side. On the right-hand side the lines have been indented and thus the crayon will go over them, leaving them white against a dark background. On the left-hand side the lines are slightly raised and thus attract a heavier coating of crayon than the background.

Conté works well for this technique, though it is also possible to use charcoal, pencil, and pastels. If a crayon is used it should be applied lightly and evenly in several directions, so that the strength of shading is built up gradually.

45

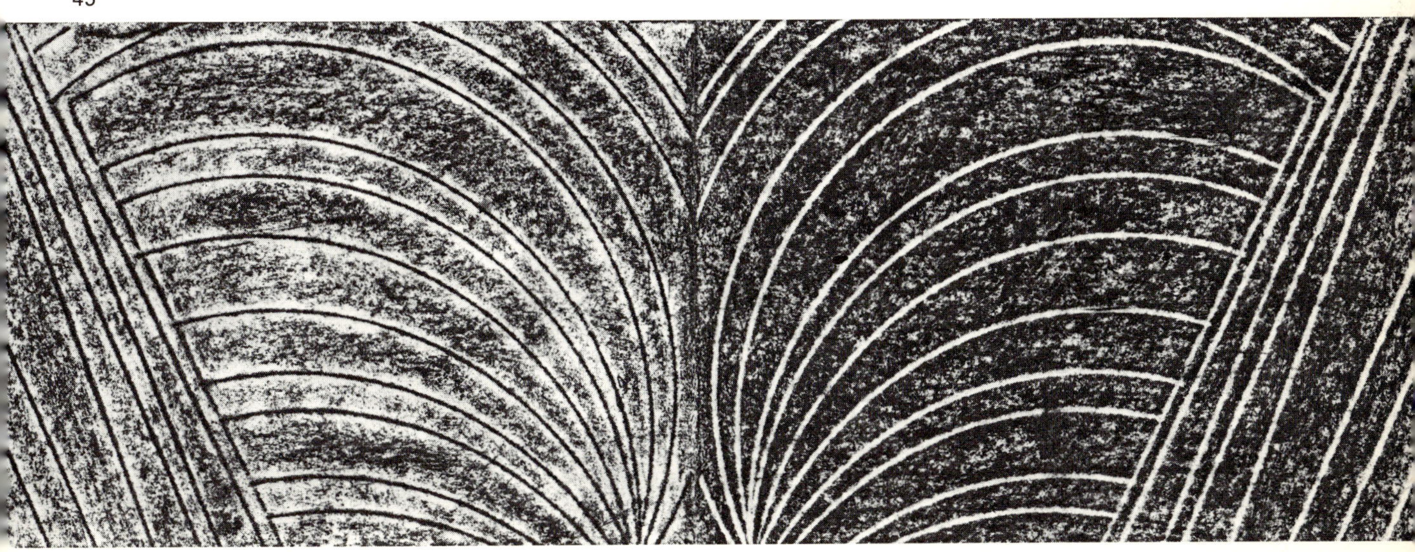

Erased line

As illustrated in figure 46, an eraser may be used to make a drawing. The whole of the paper is first shaded in with soft pencil, applying the pencil first in one direction then in the opposite to obtain an even coating. Lines are then rubbed out, using an eraser against a ruler or protractor or freehand.

A small eraser is the most suitable. It may be necessary to clean it occasionally by rubbing it on some scrap paper.

46

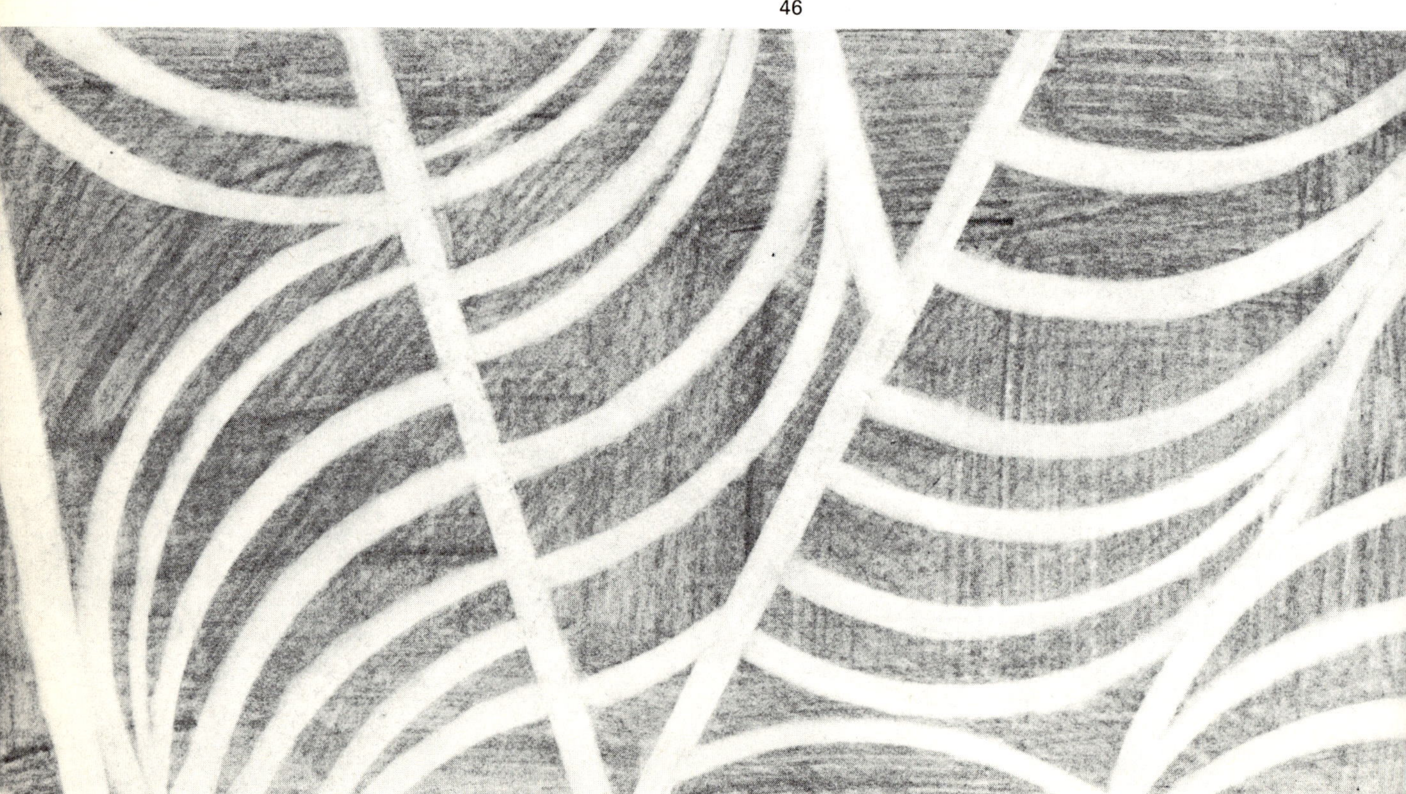

Using templates

Templates are made by cutting shapes from thin card. The shapes may then be drawn round in various positions on a sheet of paper.

Many interesting linear designs are obtainable using this method, particularly by superimposing shapes.

Figure 47 is a simple drawing in felt-tip pen, using a fish-shaped template.

In figure 48 the same template is used in four different positions.

Figure 49: the template is used in a repetitive pattern.

Figure 50: the template is overlapped.

In figure 51 rubbings of the template placed in different positions underneath the paper are made in Conté.

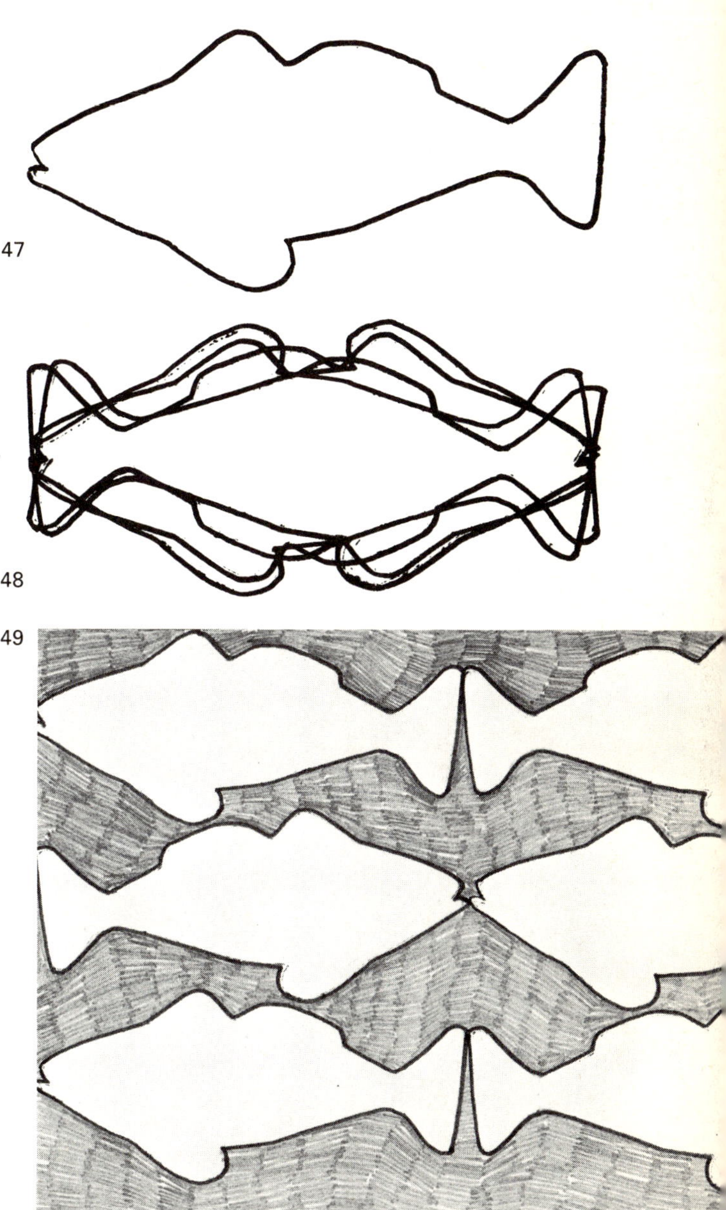

47

48

49

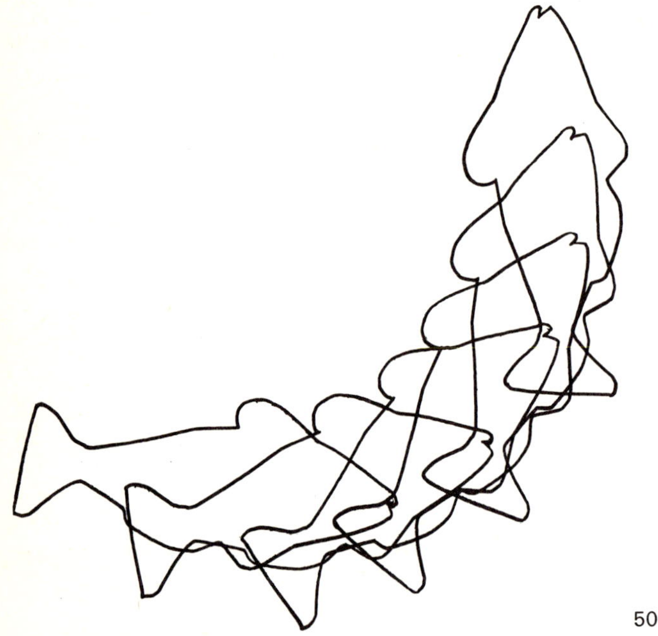

50

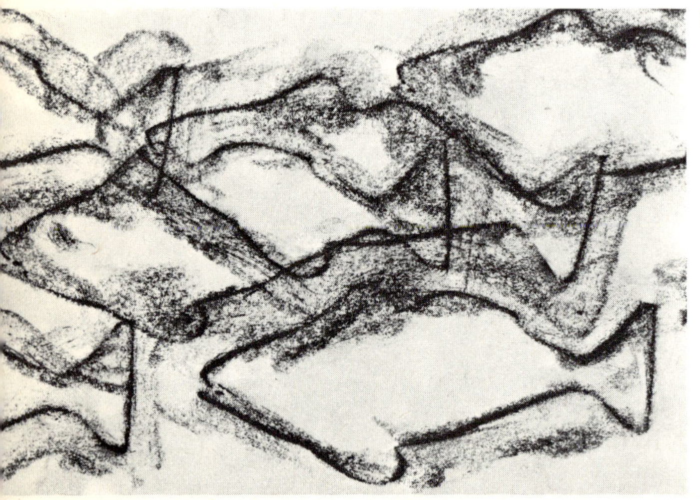

51

Edge-stencils and masking

A thin strip of paper or card can be used as an edge-stencil when drawing. The strip may have shapes cut from it, as in figure 52. In this example alternate spaces have been filled in, creating a lively positive/negative design. In figure 53 the triangular shapes were built up by using a thin strip of paper as an edge-stencil. The strip was placed in position on the paper and lines drawn down one edge of it for the desired length. The short, hatched lines begin on the strip and are made to run on to the drawing paper for about 5 mm ($\frac{1}{4}$ in.). The strokes should be quite close together, and result in an interesting broken line. The paper strip is then removed and placed in different positions and other shapes are built up in this way.

In figure 54 a torn strip of paper has been used in different positions to mask out sections of continuous lines. A ruler was used, the pencil lines starting on the drawing paper, running across the mask strip, and then on to the drawing paper again. Lines are drawn across the whole of the strip in this way and result in a silhouetted shape when it is eventually removed.

In figure 55 the paper was first folded into eight equal strips. During the drawing the paper was folded back in various ways so that certain parts were masked out.

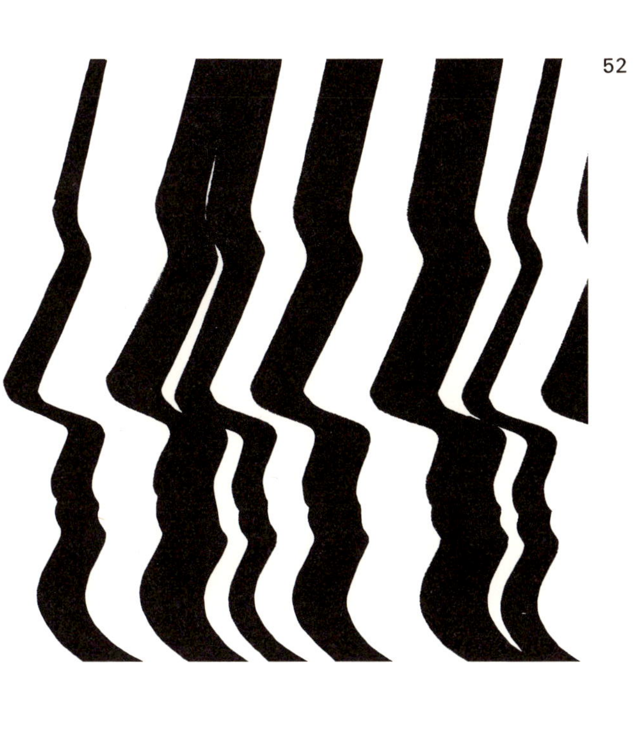

52 53

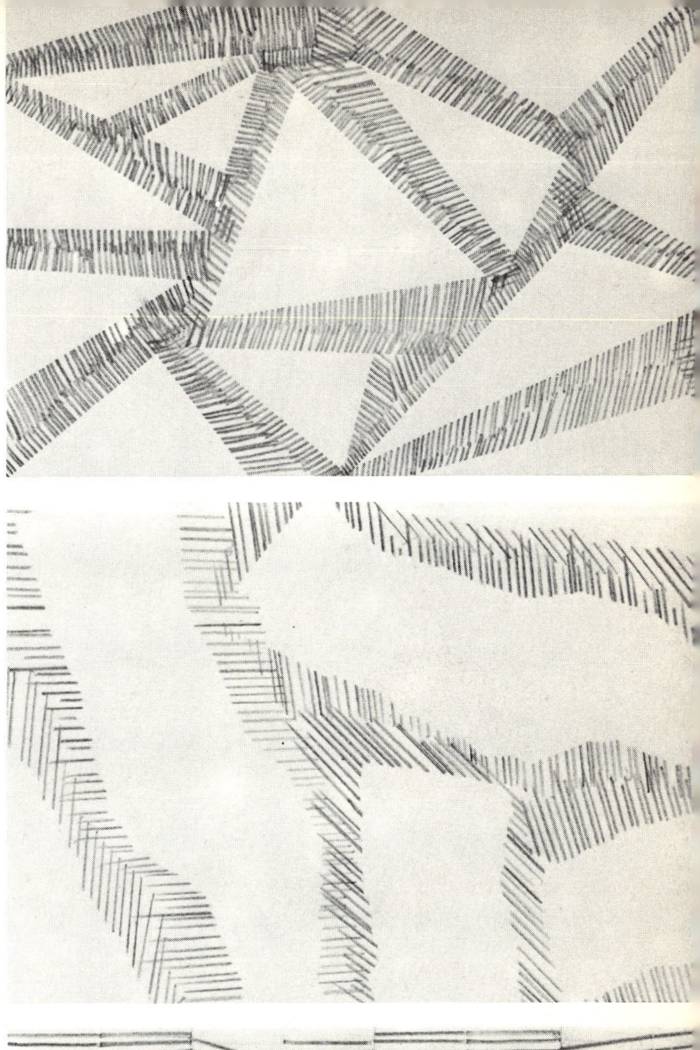

54

55

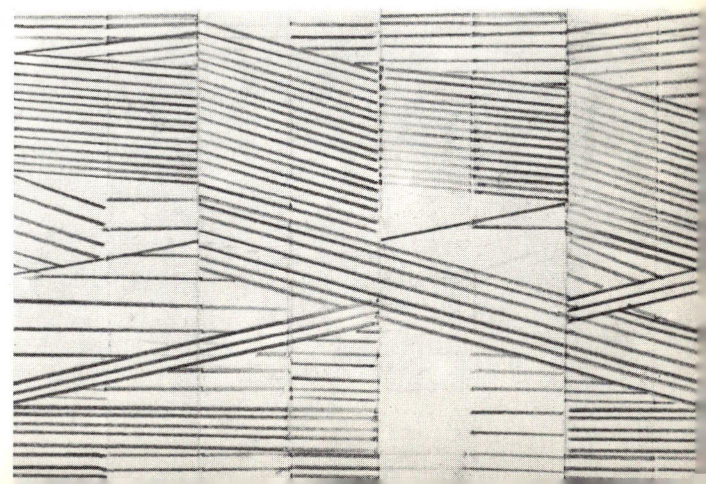

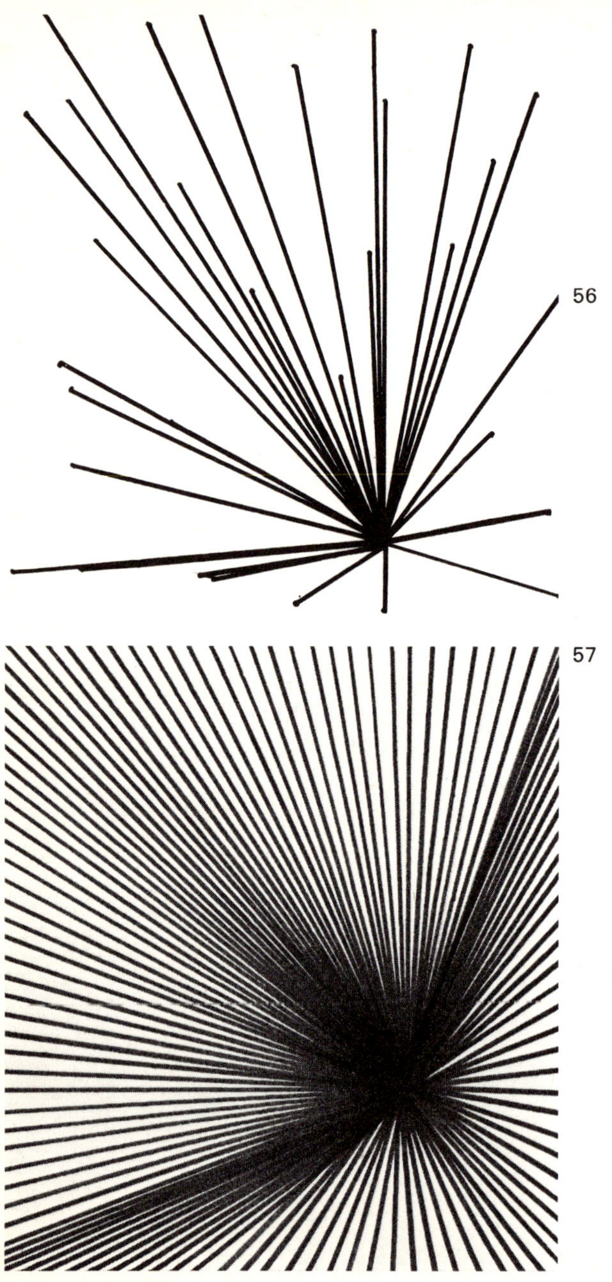

56

57

Joining dots

Dots placed at random or at determined intervals can make an effective foundation for a drawing. In figure 56 dots made at random have been joined to a common point. Similarly dots can be joined so as to form a continuous line.

Figures 57 and 58 both use dots spaced at equal intervals along all four edges of the drawing paper. These have been joined to common points.

These drawings need to be of a small scale; accuracy and neatness are essential. The shape of the drawing paper can play its part in the result; a rectangular shape, if divided up, will give a totally different effect to that of a square. Numerous variations are possible.

58

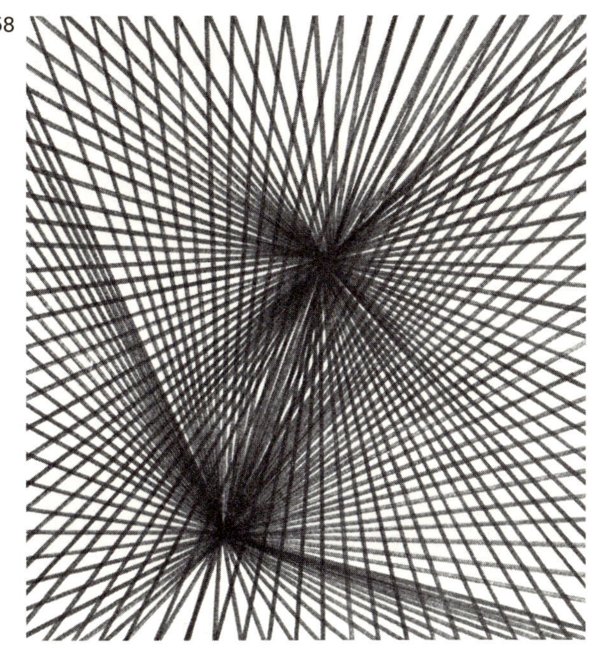

Duplicate images

Several drawing instruments may be used at once. It is essential that they are held firmly so that they maintain their relationship to each other. Two, three, four or even more pencils, felt-tip pens, ball-points or other tools may be held in the hand together and a drawing made. A combination of different drawing tools may add to the effect.

In figure 59 two felt-tip pens were used.

59

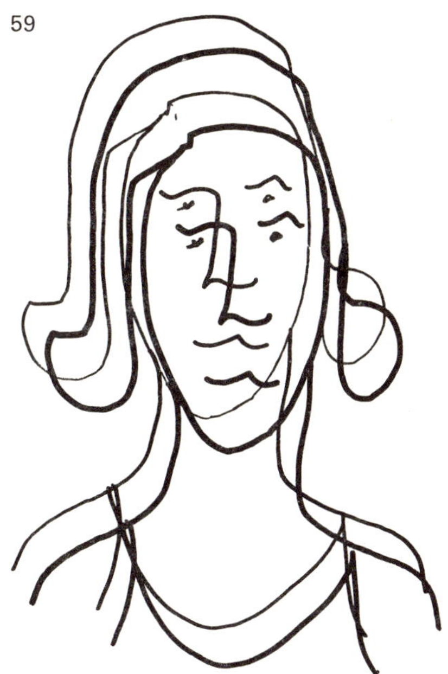

Typed designs

Remarkable results can be produced with a typewriter. Selected letters or symbols may be used to build up a design, involving various movements and spacings as well as capital and lower case letters. A certain proficiency in using the typewriter may be necessary with more complex designs.

In figure 60 the repetition of a single letter forms an attractive symmetrical design.

60

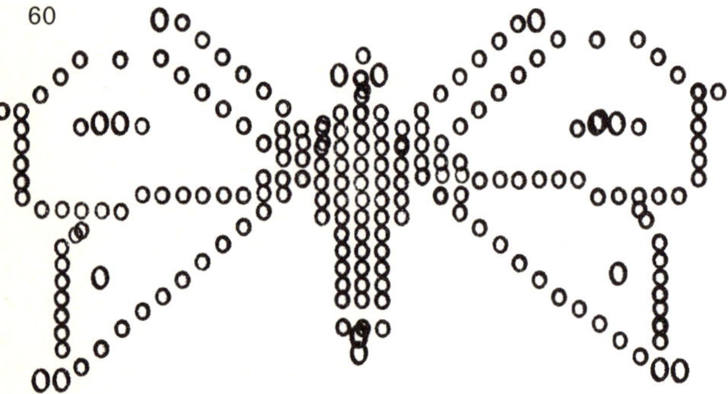

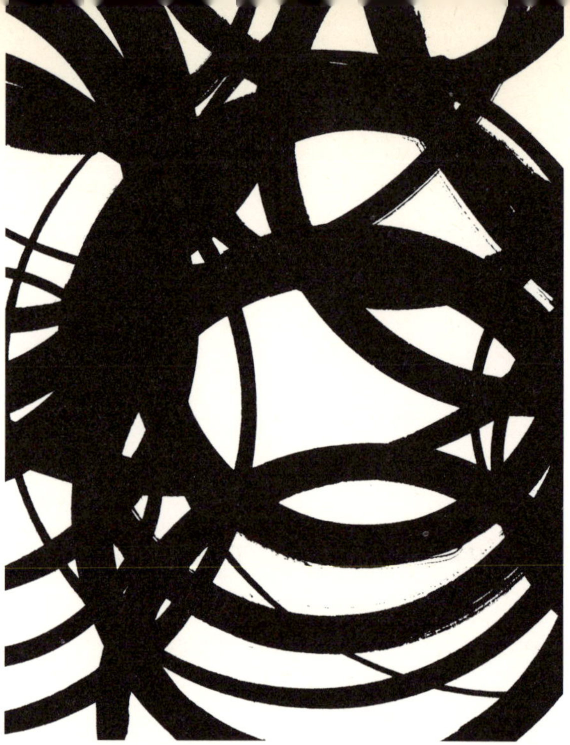

61

62

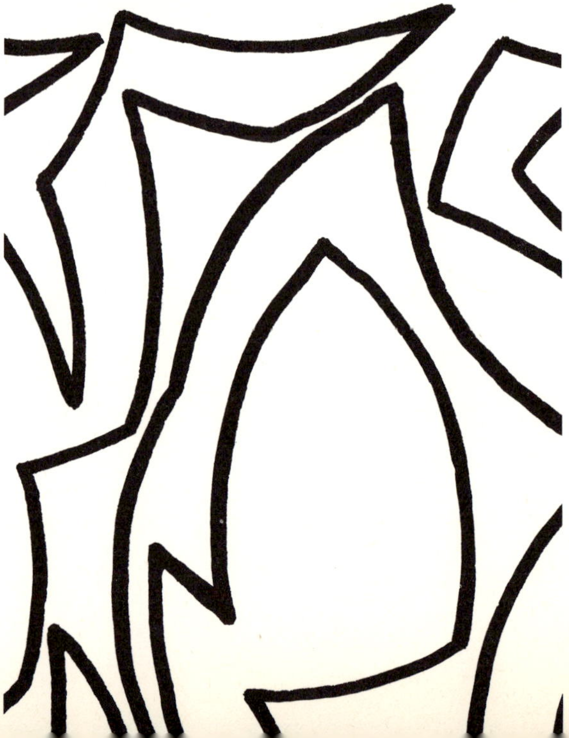

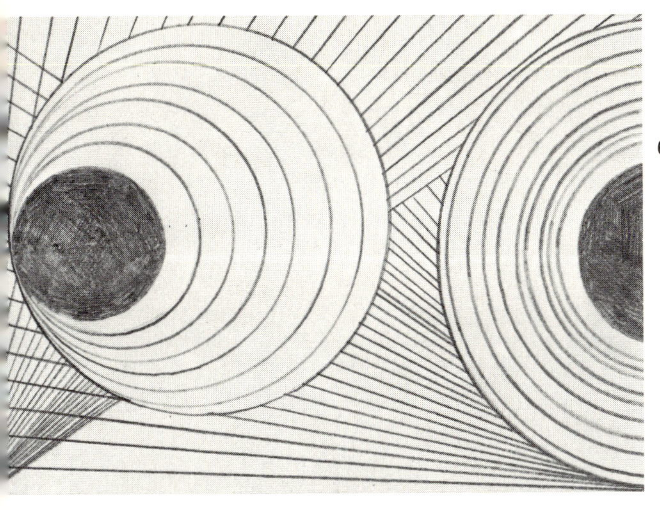

63

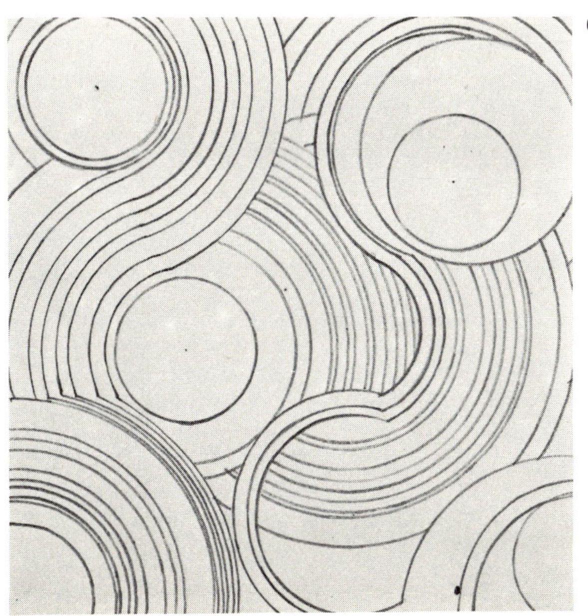

64

Using a compass

As well as its direct use for creating designs, the compass can be employed in conjunction with other techniques such as wax-resist and templates, and over textures. The pencil is not the only drawing implement that will fit into a compass and experiments can be made using other drawing tools and media.

In figure 61 a brush was used, being charged periodically with indian ink. Varying pressure on the brush produced circles of different thickness.

The compass will also describe arcs, and these may be linked together in various ways, perhaps using straight lines, or as in figure 62, by joining the arcs together to form lines.

A combination of arcs and circles can be used, as in figure 64, or circles with other lines and shapes. Some areas can be shaded in, as in figure 63.

Again, a combination of media in the making of one drawing may produce more interesting results.

Pencils, coloured pencils, charcoal pencils, charcoal, chalk, ball-points, felt-tip pens and wax crayons are among other drawing media which can be used in a compass.

Linear abstract

Infinite variations are possible for linear abstract drawings. Many of the ideas already described and illustrated may be used to this end. Pure abstract drawing involves the use of a straight-edge, compass, or both and may, as in figure 65, incorporate two or more media. Alternatively, abstract shapes may be drawn freehand, as in the work of the artist Joan Miró.

Another idea for linear abstract work is to repeat or build from a shape, which can vary in size.

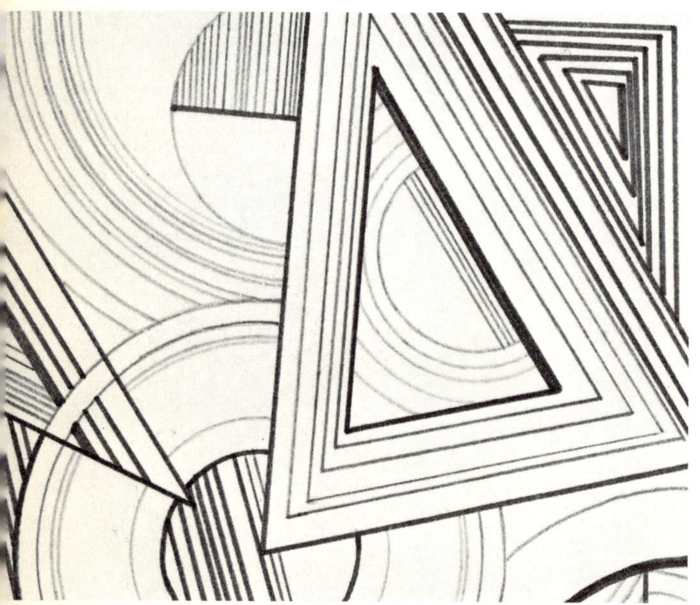

65

Linear decorative

Shapes may be subdivided in many different ways, and each of the resulting shapes decorated by various forms of line. See figure 66.

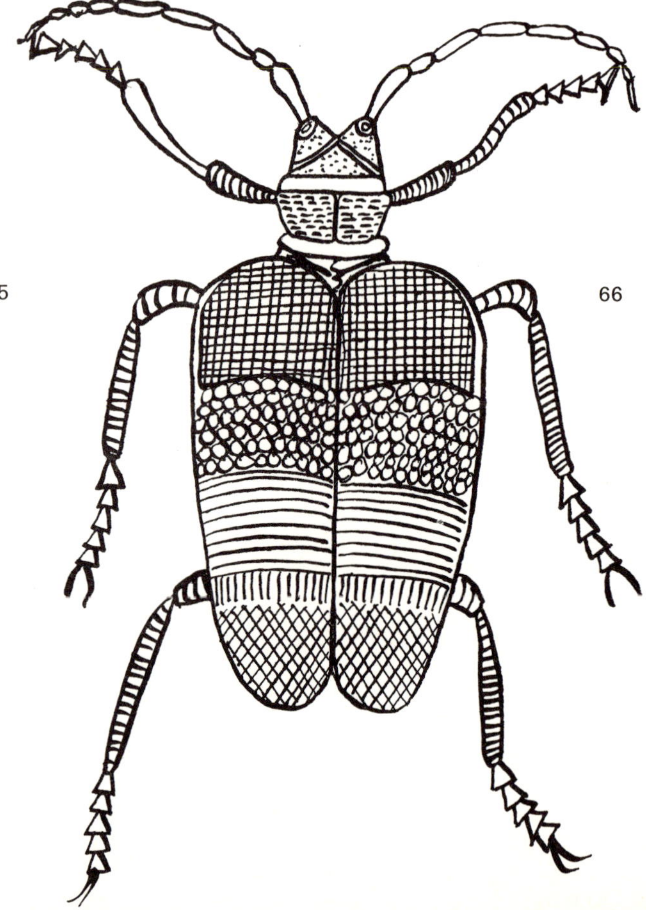

66

Line drawings

The use of pure line can produce the most powerful and expressive drawing. A few simple lines can convey a great deal, and the linear technique is therefore well suited to drawings of life, still-life or landscape, see figures 67 to 70.

Figure 70 shows how guide lines may be used in the plotting of a drawing, particularly, as in this case, if it is of a symmetrical object. As illustrated, the drawing of the object may be constructed around a centre guide line. Distances may then be checked from this line. Guide lines are normally erased before the drawing is completed. Lines may also be used to divide up areas and form the equivalent of areas of tone. A variation in their spacing will create different intensities and may help in the 'modelling' of a particular object.

The guide lines in figure 69 have been left to form an integral part of the drawing, giving an interesting semi-abstract result.

Lines may be drawn in many other ways, though it is not possible within the limitations of this book to detail these. Lines may be engraved into clay and wood, for example, and linear designs constructed with string and thread.

67

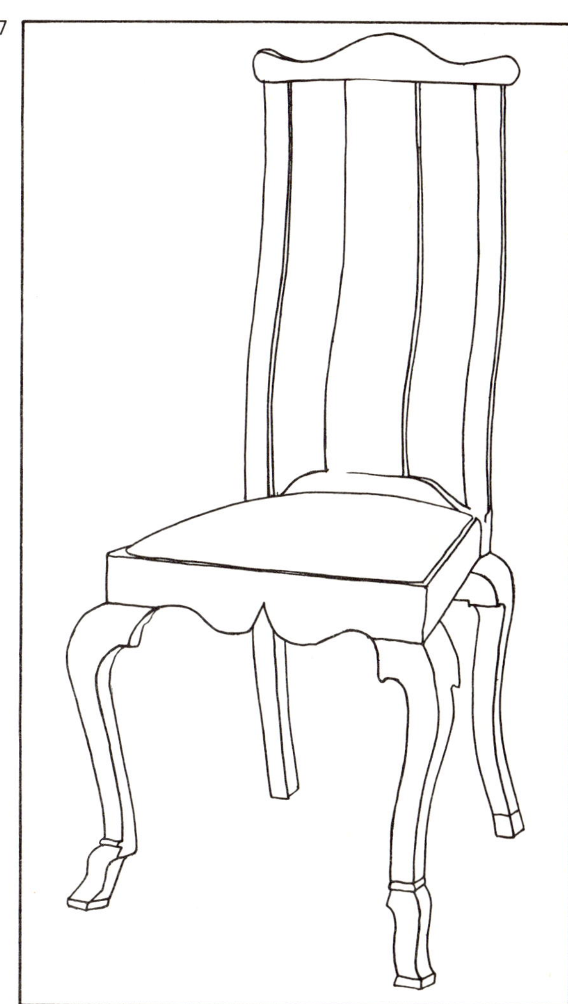

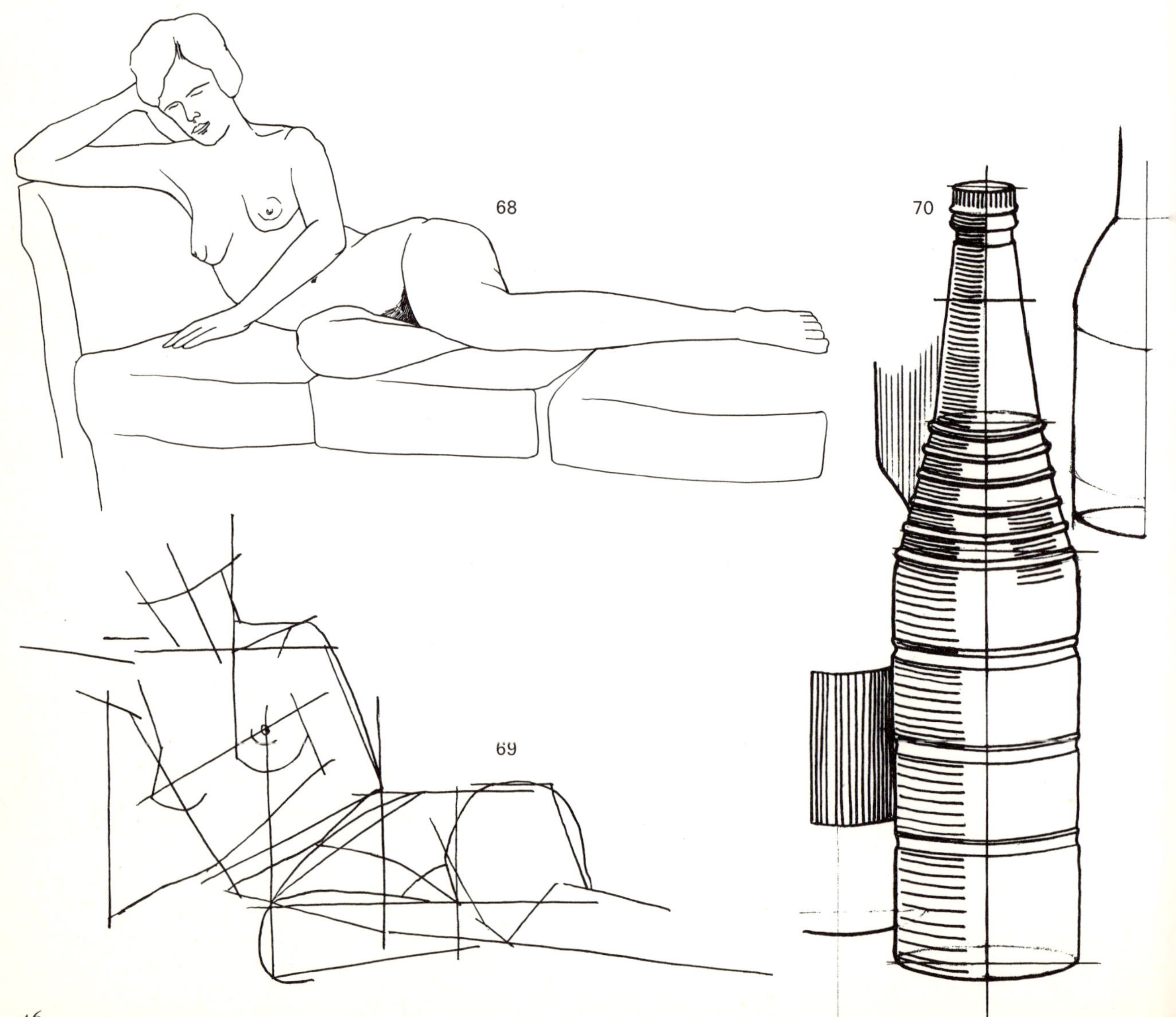
68
69
70

Point

Drawings can be built up from dots or points applied in a variety of ways. A number of artists, among them Picasso, Matisse, Signac, Seurat and Van Gogh, have employed a 'pointillist' technique in some of their work, and a study of these will serve to illustrate techniques as well as inspire others.

As with other methods different kinds of implements may be used to make drawings from point. Felt-tip pens, ball-points and pencils are the most obvious, but points can also be offset with fingers, dowelling and the ends of pencils or paint brushes. Point may be dropped, sprayed or flicked; designs may be built up with stamped point or they can be typed. Often interesting results will be achieved by combining point of different sizes, as well as making contrasts in the spacing and intensity of the points.

Most drawings will be made on cartridge (drawing) paper, though experiments can be made with papers of various textures and colours. The size of the drawings should relate to the technique and the implements being used. On the whole for this method, drawing on a small scale, say 200 mm × 200 mm (8 in. × 8 in.), is recommended.

Many of the ideas illustrated in the section on line may equally well be carried out by the use of point. Rather than repeat all of these here, this section concentrates on ideas and techniques which relate more specifically to the use of point.

GEORGES SEURAT: *Entrance to the Port of Honfleur, 1886* (detail)
Oil. Philadelphia

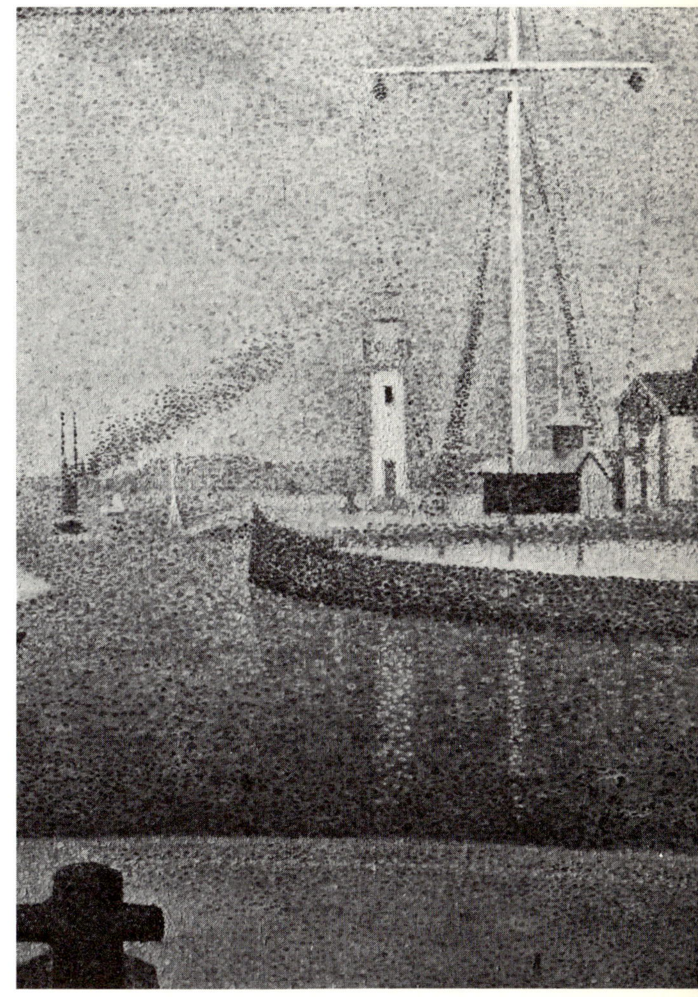

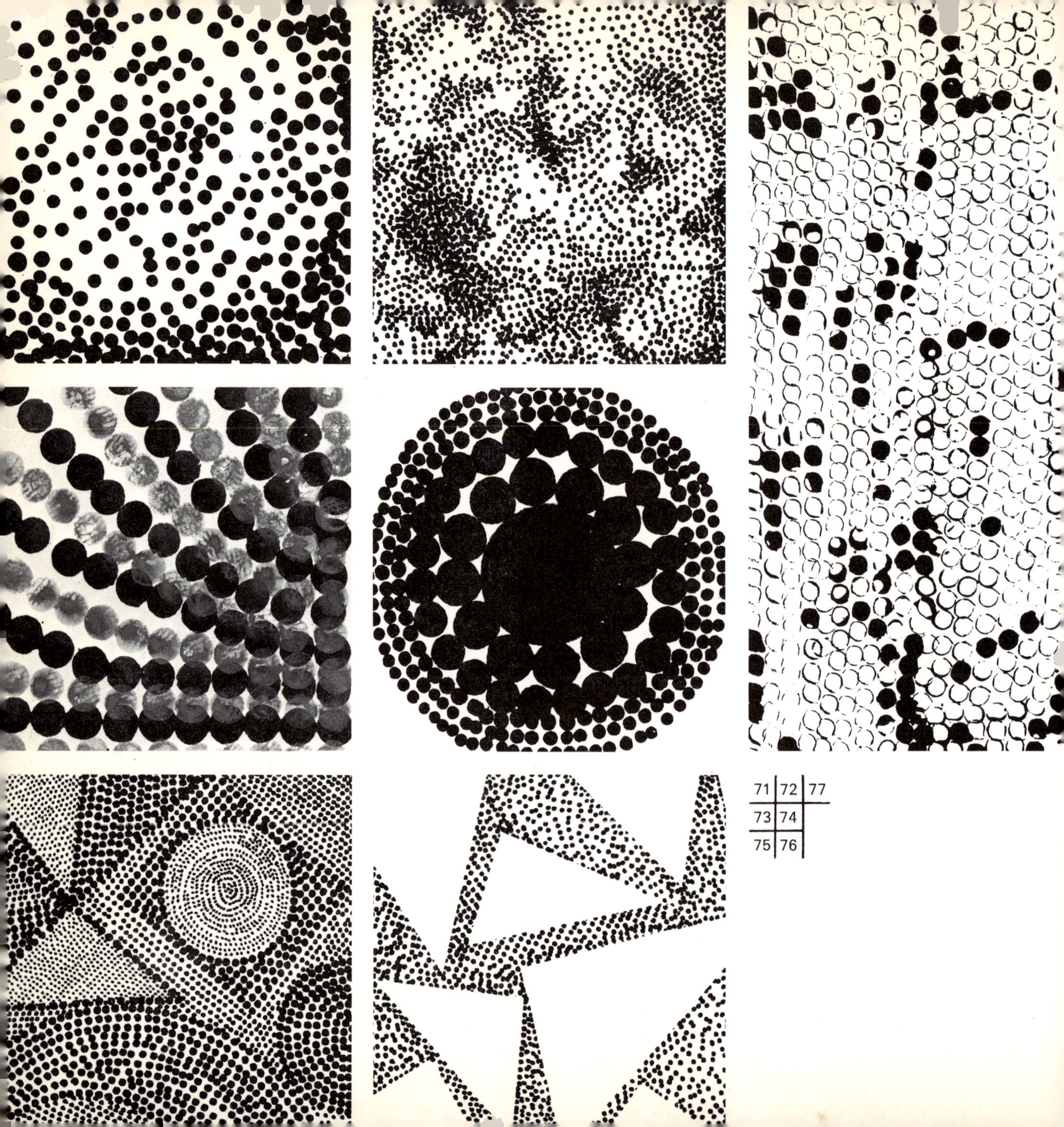
71 72 77
73 74
75 76

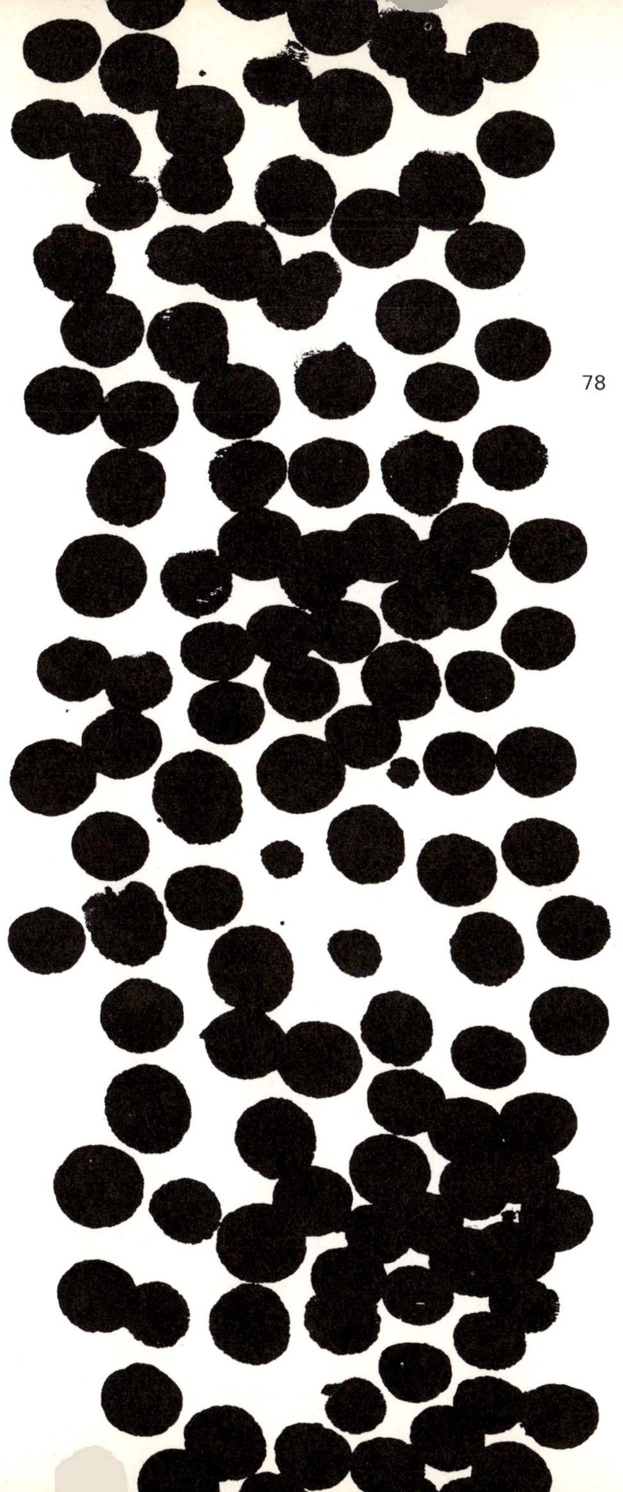

Offset and impressed point

78 A variety of implements, dipped in ink or paint, may be used to offset points. Different sizes of dowelling, as well as the flat ends of pencils and paint brushes, are the most useful.

With all techniques involving offsetting it is important to realise that only the end of the implement needs to be dipped into the paint or ink before transferring it to the drawing paper. If the length of dowelling or other tool being used is immersed to any depth it becomes difficult to control the result. A palette or other container with a very shallow covering of paint or ink is therefore required.

In figure 71 three paint brushes, each of a different size, were used to create a design with a concentration of point towards the edges. The flat, wooden ends of the brushes were dipped in indian ink.

Figure 72 is a drawing with a felt-tip pen and shows how grouping can produce effective contrasts within the design.

Other contrasts may be obtained by combining different tones or colours, as in figure 73, or by using point of various sizes, figures 74 and 75. In figure 75 felt-tip pens have been used, while in figure 74 different sizes of dowelling have been employed.

Impressed point may be used to carry out many of the ideas mentioned in the section on line. Figure

76 illustrates the use of point and a strip of paper used to mask out, see also figures 53 and 54.

Other objects may be used to impress point on to a sheet of paper. In figure 77 a drinking-straw has been used. This was first dipped into some ink and then pressed on to the paper. Several images can be made before it becomes necessary to dip the drinking-straw into the ink again. Here, the contrast between full shapes and weaker ones can be exploited to add to the interest of the design.

In figure 78 the design has been made by the accumulation of points which were offset in paint with a finger. Paint of a medium consistency was used and variations in the pressure of the finger resulted in points of different sizes.

Stamped point

Interesting results can be obtained by using the small circles made by a paper punch. These are arranged on a sheet of paper of a suitably contrasting colour and glued in the desired positions.

Circles may be punched from papers of many different colours and textures. It is also possible to punch the circles from gummed paper which eases the problem of gluing. Otherwise, clear paper glue should be used. It should be applied very sparingly; most types will dry transparent.

As an alternative, the design may be punched from the sheet of paper using a single hole punch. When completed, the paper is mounted on a sheet of a different colour. Gummed file-paper reinforcements may also be used.

Figure 79 illustrates the use of punched paper circles and gummed reinforcements.

79

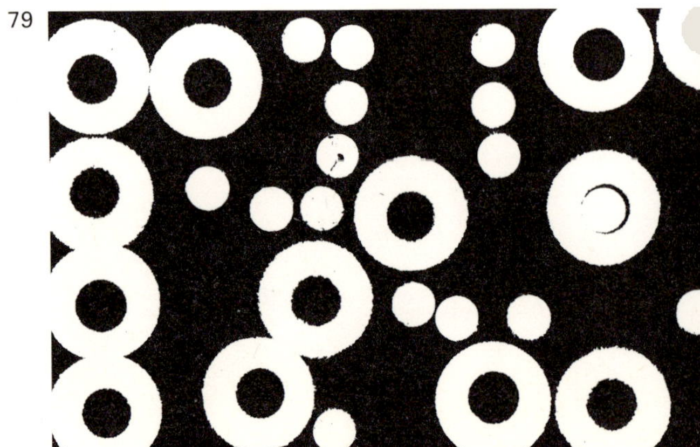

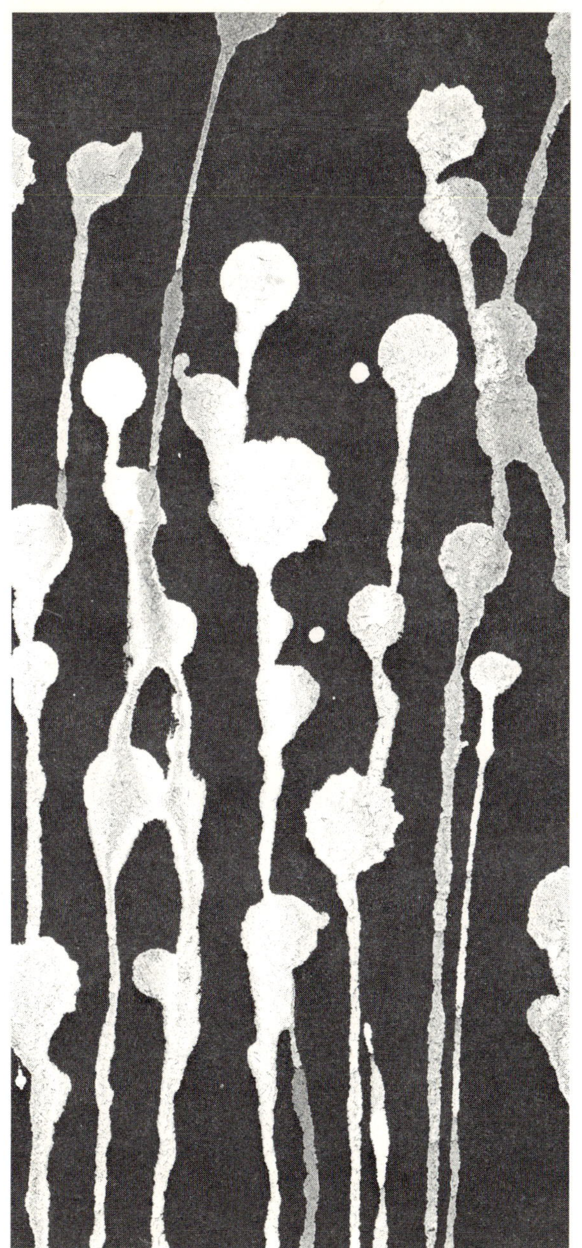

Spraying, flicking and dropping

80 Point which is applied by a spraying or flicking technique will often produce an interesting textured ground on which more conventional drawings can be made. Simple linear drawings, for example, are often enhanced by a textured background. Spraying, flicking and stippling techniques may also be used with templates and masking to produce effective designs. A build-up in different tones or colours, or variations in intensity of flicked or sprayed areas may also produce interesting results.

Flicked ink or paint is best applied from a fairly dry stiff-haired brush held quite near to the paper. There are two methods of flicking: the brush may be held above the paper and shaken, thus causing ink or paint to fall off on to the paper below; or the brush is held in one hand and the hairs pulled back with a finger of the other hand, this being a more controllable method. See figure 81.

In figure 82 a template has been used to mask out whilst the paper was sprayed with ink, using a spray diffuser. When the ink had dried the template was removed and the shape filled in with impressed point, using a felt-tip pen against a ruler.

'Runs' of ink or paint can also be used, see figure 80 and also figures 29 and 30. Drops of paint or ink are applied with a dropper or by holding a laden brush vertically above the paper and squeezing the hairs to force paint to drop off. Variations in the size of the drops can be achieved by changing the distance of the brush above the paper and by using brushes or droppers of different sizes.

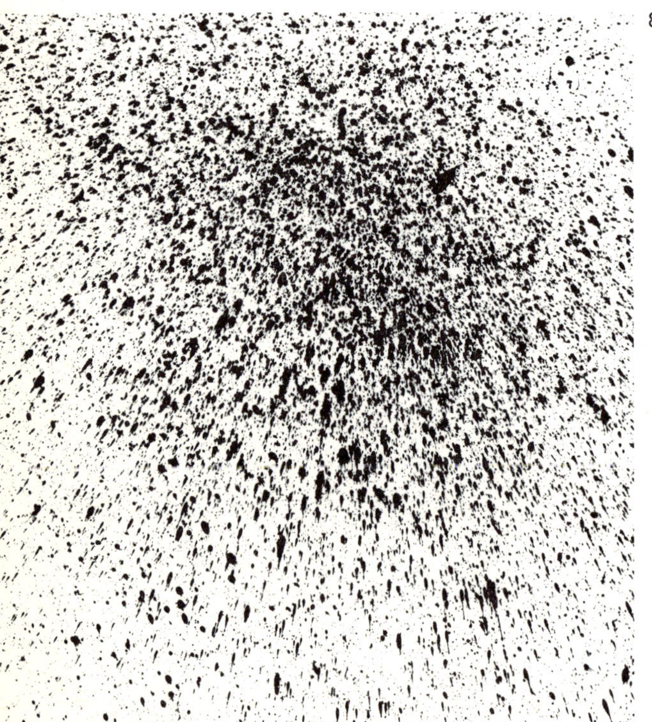

81 82

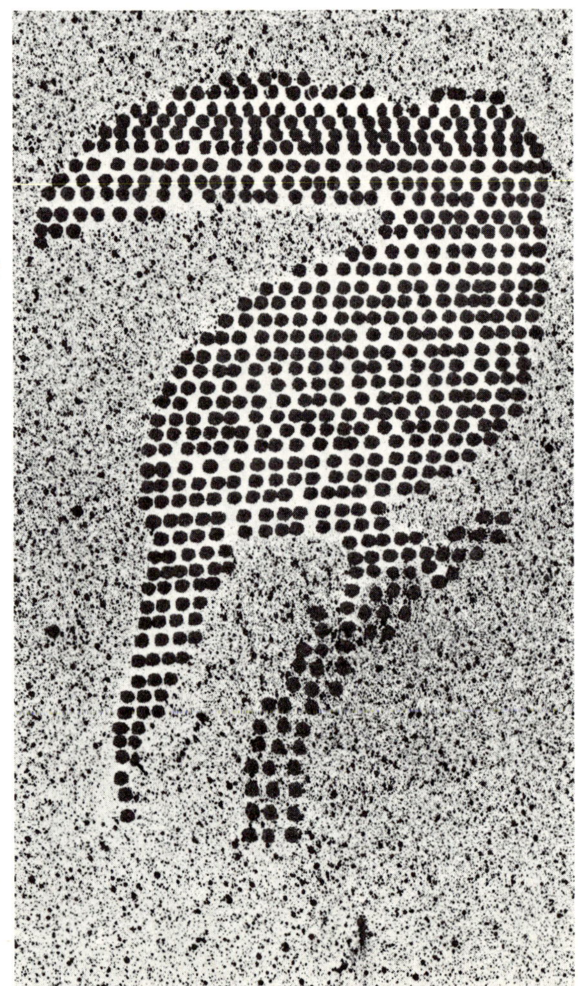

Point as a drawing technique

Subject matter may lend itself directly to a pointillist technique. Drawings may therefore be built up from points of different sizes using variations of spacing to create an impression of form.

Most drawing tools can be used, though the best results are usually obtained with pens. Figures 83 and 84 were made with a felt-tip pen. Figure 84 indicates the potential of this technique. Although they are of the same size, the accumulation of dots in certain areas creates tonal effects and the illusion of depth. These pens suit the technique well as there is a continuous flow of ink which can be easily controlled and which dries quickly. An additional advantage is that felt-tip pens are obtainable in different sizes.

Other drawings might combine the use of point with line. The drawings of Van Gogh illustrate how effectively and expressively this can be done. Point is particularly useful for breaking up an area, giving a textured effect or creating a light tone. In landscape drawings the sky can often be represented in this way, see figure 85.

83

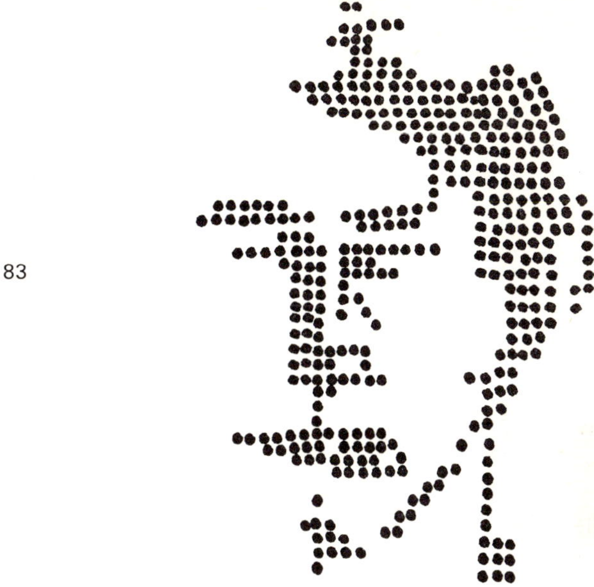

84

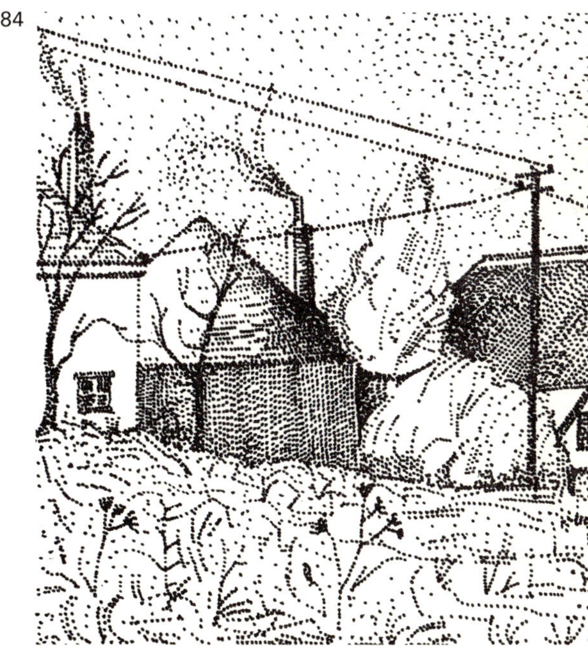

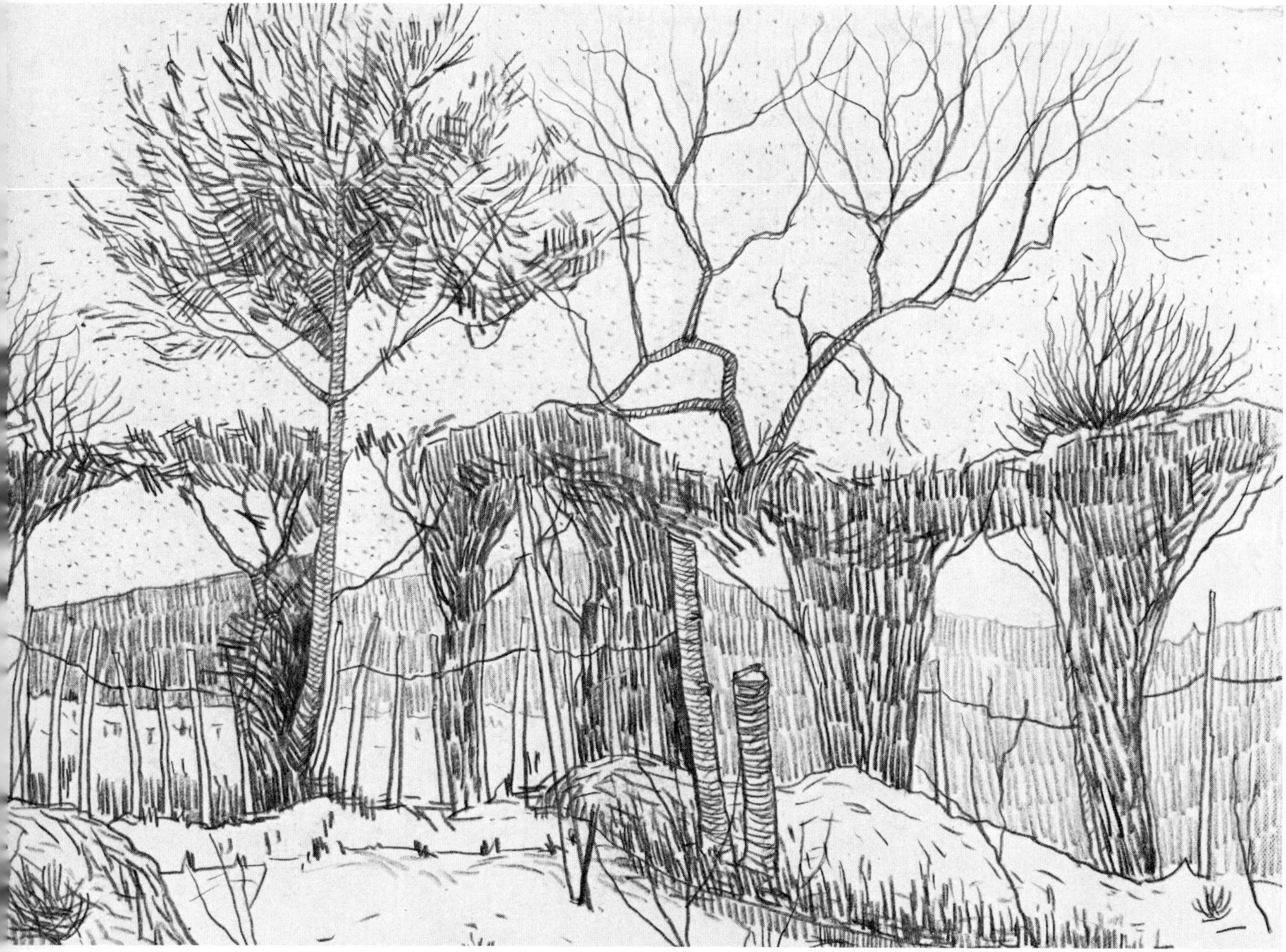

85

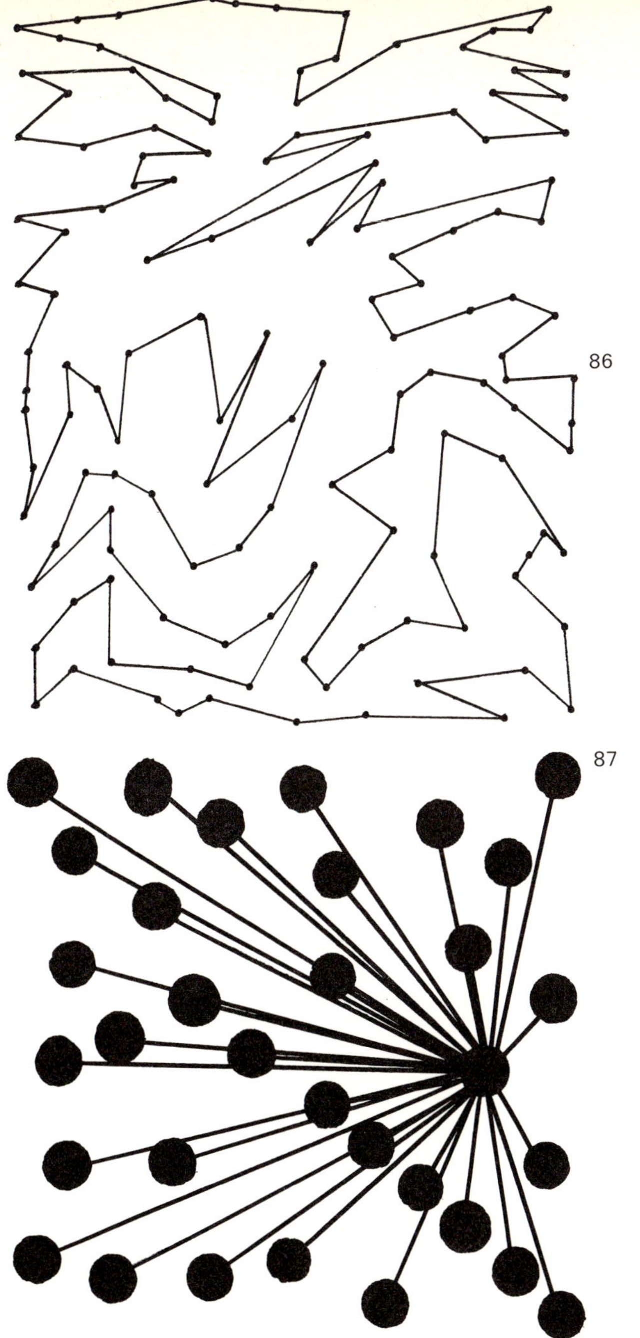

86

87

Point and line

Many of the ideas and techniques already discussed are adaptable to a combined use of point and line. This applies to both representational and pure abstract work. Joining dots is an obvious example of this combination, and two such examples are illustrated in figures 86 and 87.

88

89

Typed designs

The typewriter can be used to make designs which exploit various types of point and contrasts in spacing. Exciting, abstract 'op' designs can be made.

Copies can be taken of typed designs with carbon paper; if the carbon paper is used in reverse one can obtain a reversed image, as in figure 90.

By typing heavily an impression can be made on a second sheet of paper. This impression may be used in a similar way to a pencil impression (see figure 45) by coating it with successive layers of Conté, wax crayon, or charcoal. Such impressions will create a 'negative' of the original, as illustrated in figures 88 and 89.

Other techniques perhaps do not fall strictly within the bounds of drawing but should be mentioned. Point, for example, can be impressed into soft wood and clay; designs can be drilled into wood or punched from thin metal.

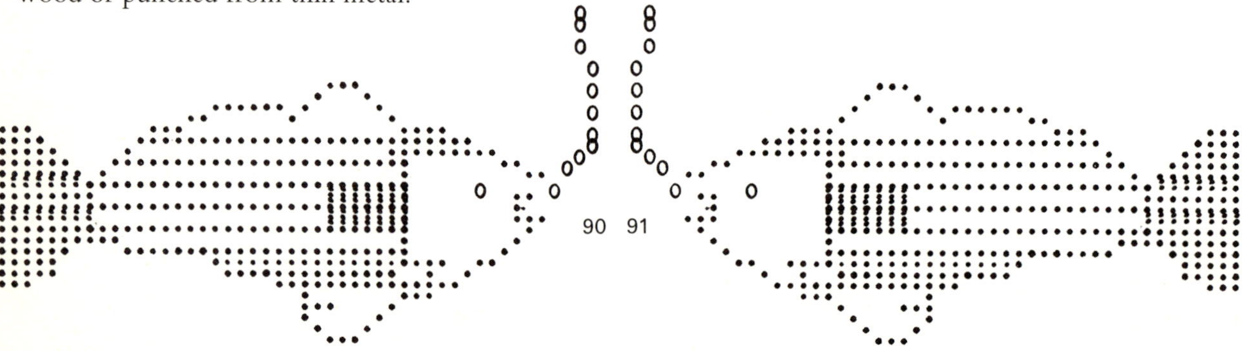
90 91

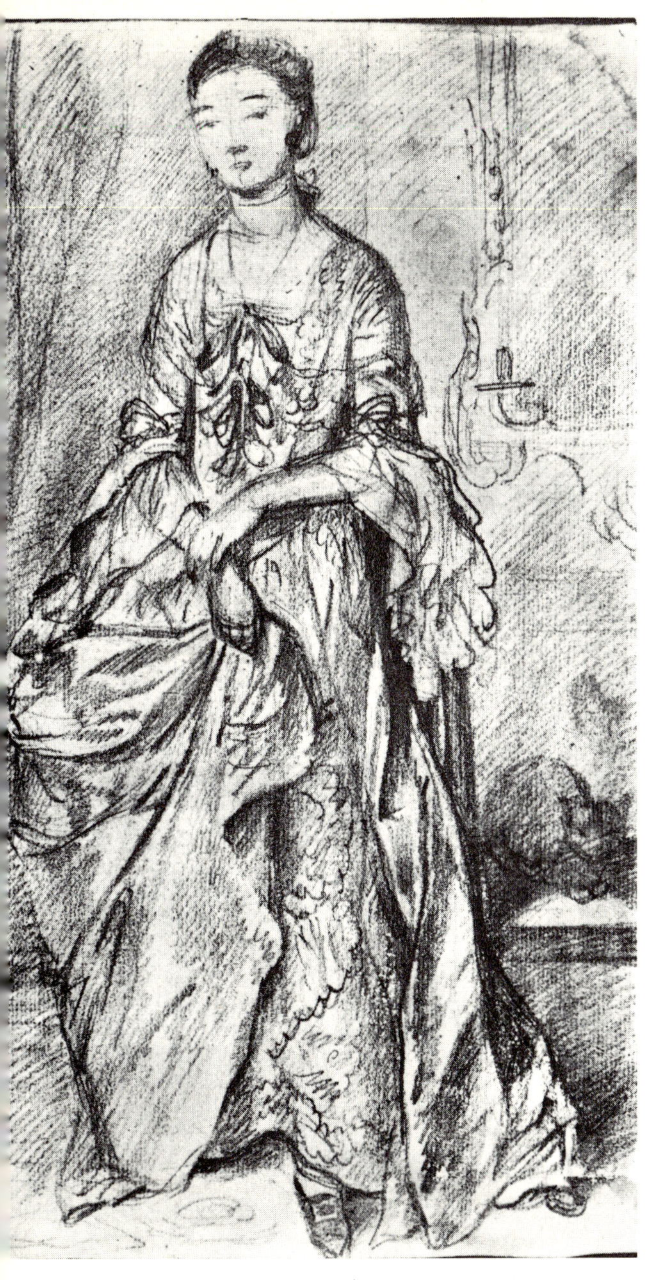

Tone

The use of tone greatly increases the possibilities that can be effected within the drawing. Contrasts of light and dark, the modelling of form, the illusion of depth, as well as the character of the subject may be achieved in this way.

Tone is essentially shading; this is normally done to create an impression of form, of solidity. There are many ways of making tonal drawings, and the artist can select the method which suits him. In some cases the technique might be suggested by the subject matter; it will also be affected by the experience of the artist and his emotional response to what he is drawing.

Again experiments should be made with a wide range of drawing tools and media. Changes of tone may be achieved by using different media within the one drawing. Variations in pressure with the drawing tool can also effect tonal contrasts.

Preliminary exercises to exploit the character

THOMAS GAINSBOROUGH: *Study of a woman standing in an interior, with a cat seated on a chair beside her*
Pencil. Victoria and Albert Museum
Crown copyright

and possibilities of a particular medium will give confidence and serve as a useful introduction to more complex work.

Figures 92 to 94 show exercises involving variations of pressure and experiments with different media.

92

93 94

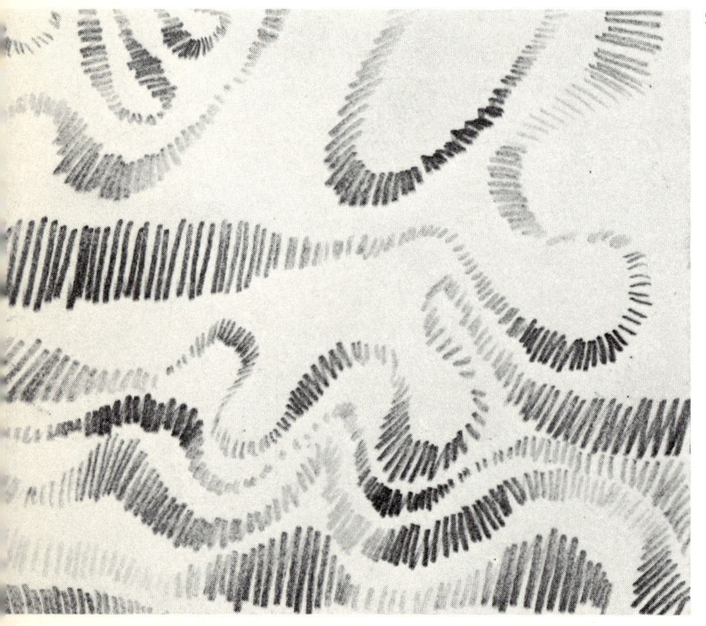

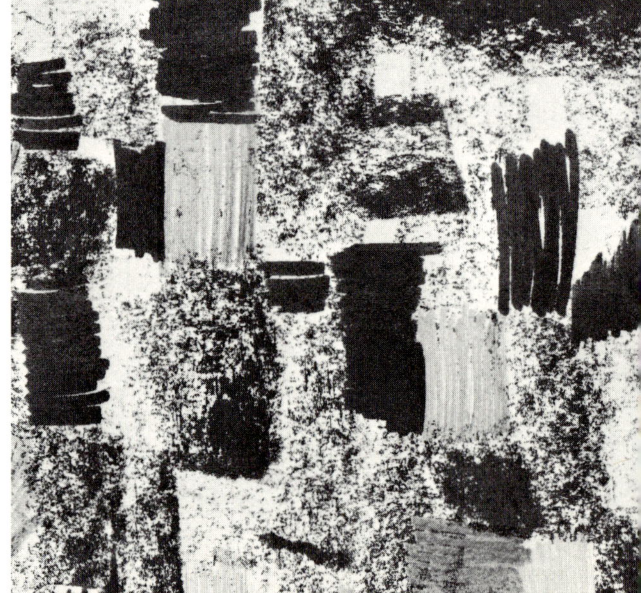

Linear tone

It has already been noted that lines grouped together can give a tonal impression, see page 45. There are various ways of doing this: the pressure or spacing may vary, the lines may be short (hatched) or long, they may be drawn freehand or ruled, they may be superimposed by others in a

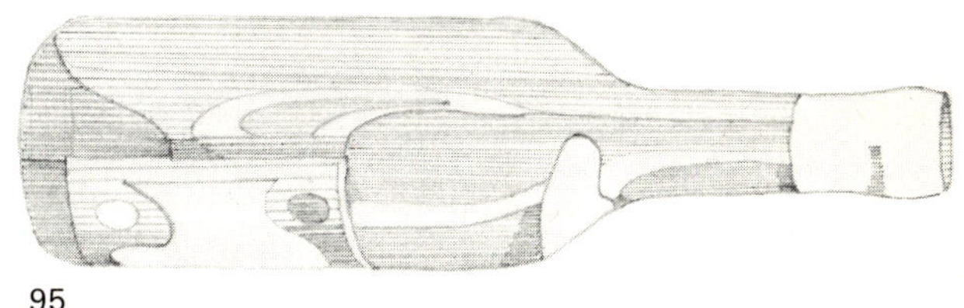

95

96

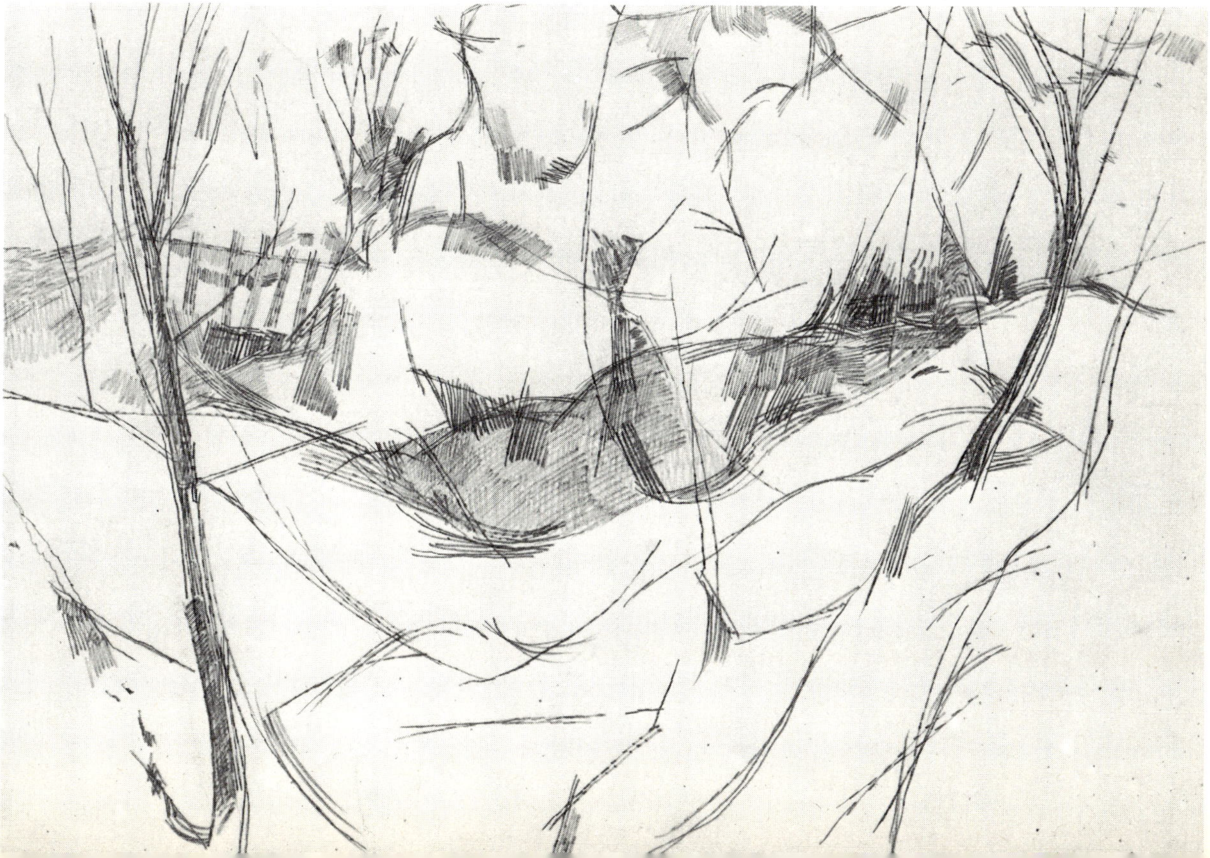

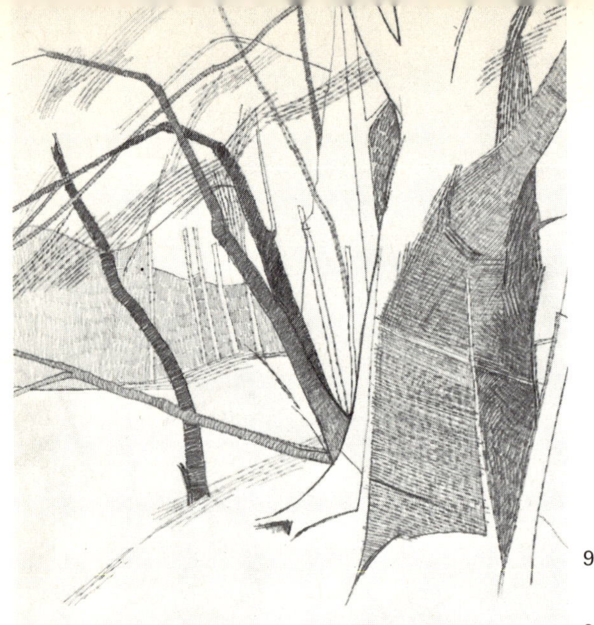

97

different direction (cross-hatched), and combinations both of techniques and media may be used. In this instance the shapes within the drawing are being subdivided into a series of smaller areas by the application of line. By its nature this produces a very stylised form of drawing, but with skill

98

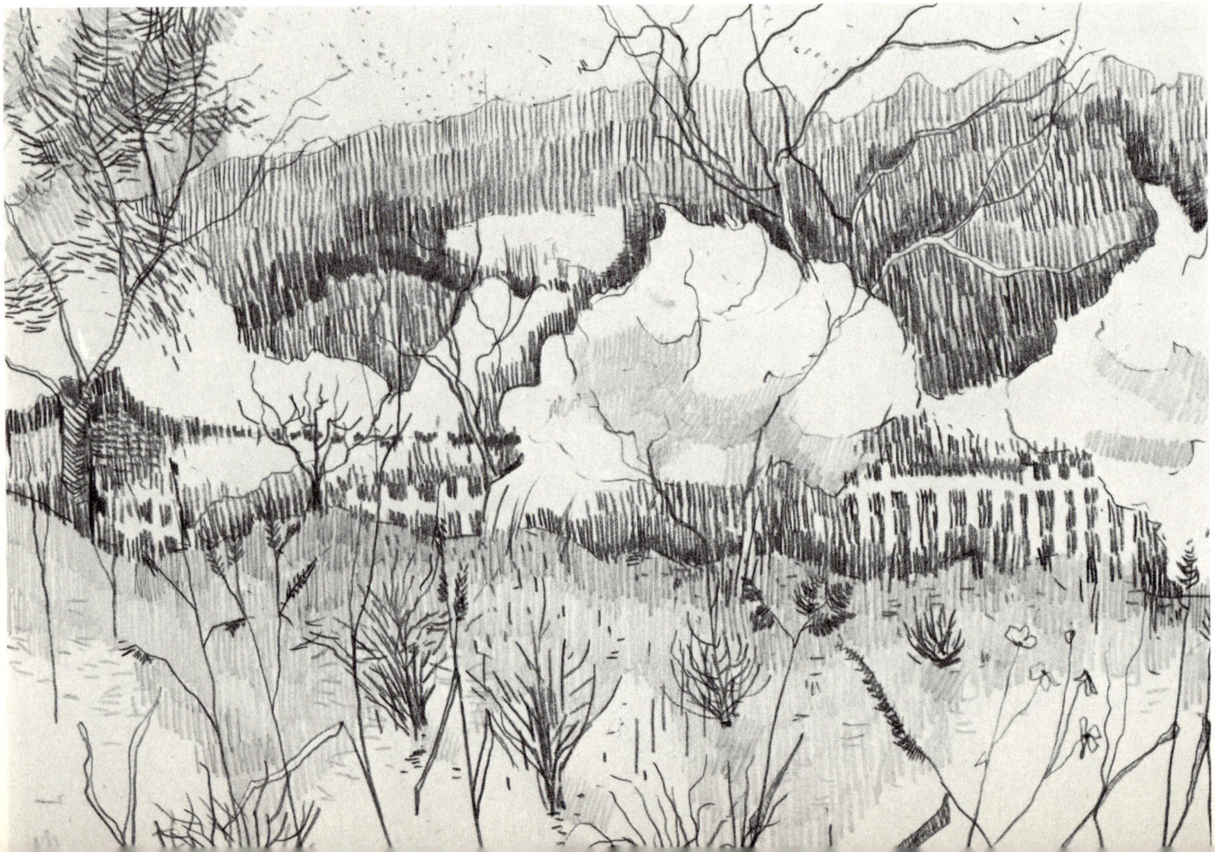

subtle changes from light to dark are possible. Eighteenth and nineteenth century etchings illustrate these linear techniques very well.

Some of the ways of using lines with varying pressure are illustrated in figures 95 to 97.

Figure 96 is a landscape sketch where groups of lines are used to build up areas of tone. The drawing was made with a pencil; the lines are of different strengths, they are sometimes superimposed, and are drawn freehand. As in this example, it is possible to achieve variations of tone even within the length of a single line. See also figure 92.

99

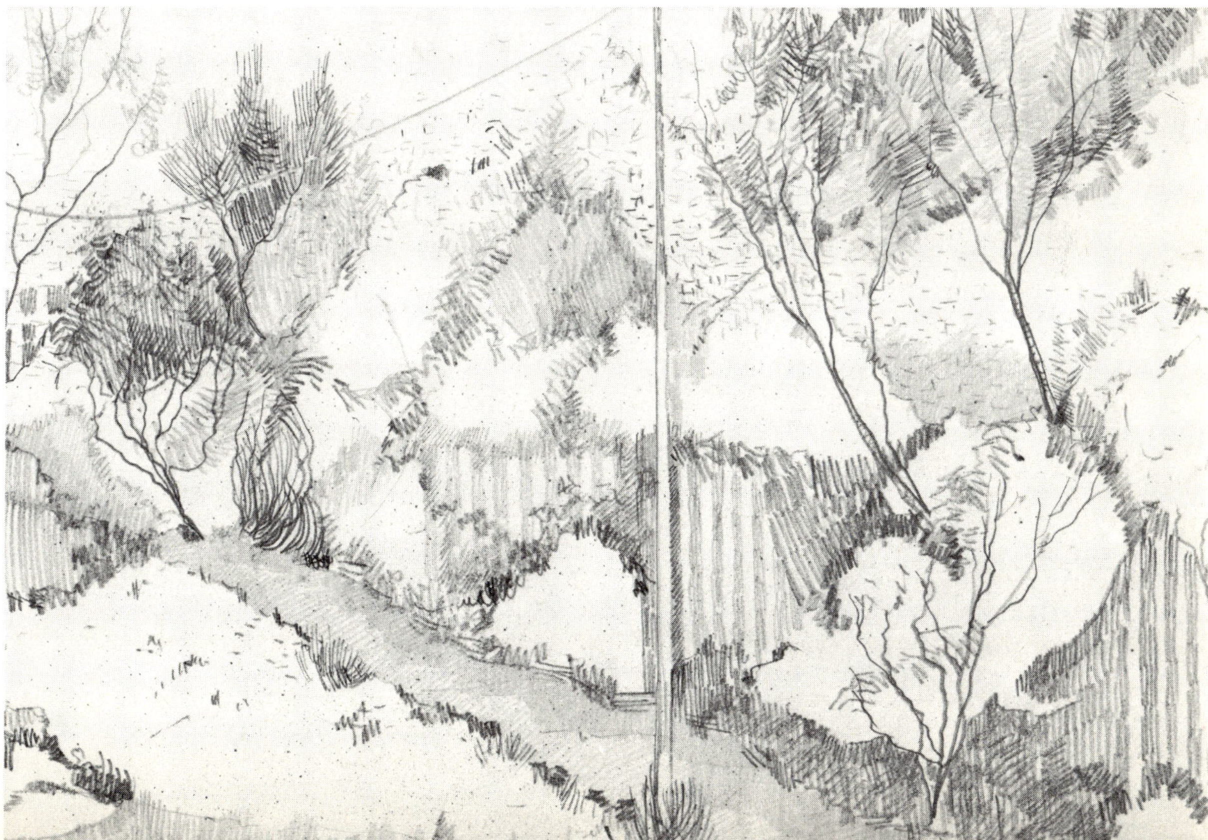

In figure 95 shapes are subdivided by ruled lines. Lines closer together will give the illusion of a stronger tone than those drawn at wider intervals, even though the lines may all be of equal strength.

Figure 97 shows a more organised division and subdivision by lines which vary in strength, spacing and length.

The use of hatched line is shown in figures 98 to 101. Hatched lines are usually short and produce work of a vital, lively character, as can be seen in many of the drawings of Van Gogh. Again, tonal effects are created by differences in spacing or pressure, or possibly, as in figure 98, by employing different media. Hatching does not have to be bold; a more subtle use is illustrated in figure 99. Existing lines may be shaded over with others in a different direction to give more solid areas of tone, a technique known as cross-hatching. Gradations of shading can be made in this way. Areas of tone may consist of several layers of lines using this technique, so that eventually a solid shape is formed with no hint of the linear way in which it was obtained. Similarly edges can be 'lost' by a gradual

100

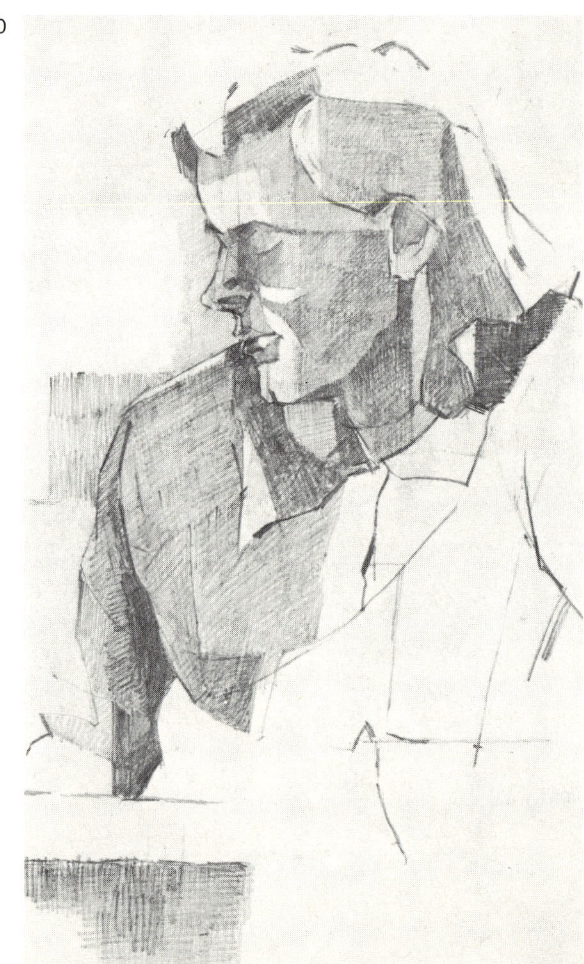

fading out of cross-hatched lines. Tones made in this way are often used in combination with hatched and single lines, see figure 101.

Shading can also be made by a scribble method, applied with a circular motion or continuous line technique.

101

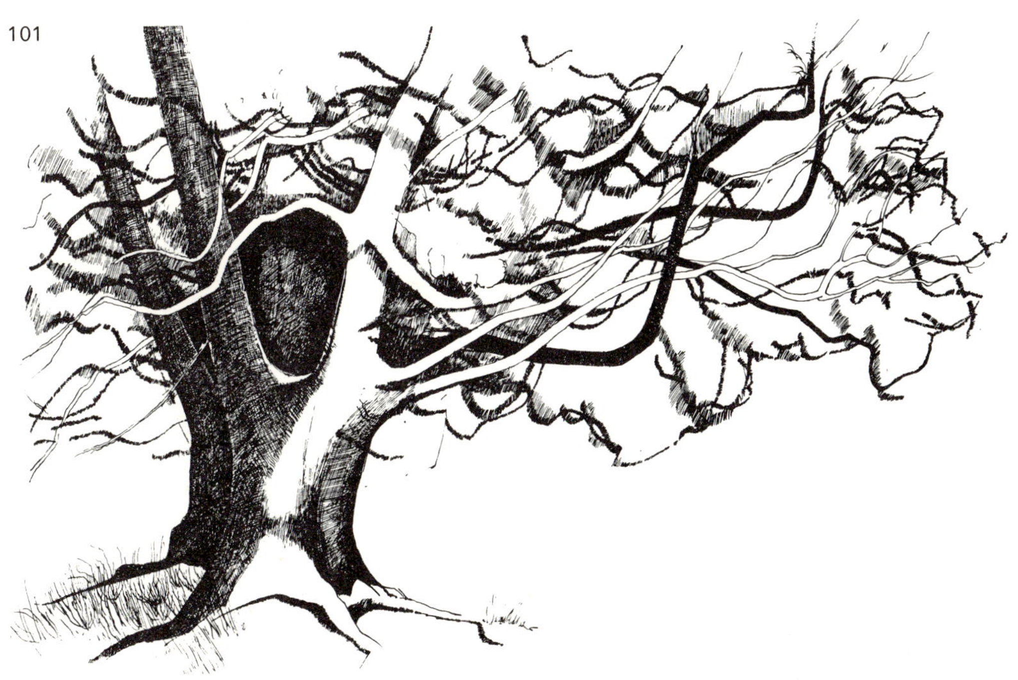

Offset tone

Some of the most subtle tonal effects are obtained by offsetting, or by techniques involving smearing, smudging or rubbing.

The gradual transition of tone from light to dark was once regarded as essential to good drawing. Leonardo da Vinci said that light and shadows should blend 'without lines or borders, in the manner of smoke'. During the period of the High Renaissance the technique of shading known as sfumato was developed. Sfumato comes from the Italian word 'sfumare', meaning to evaporate, and is used to describe the transitions of tone by such gradual stages as to be indiscernible.

To achieve such 'vaporose' effects a soft drawing medium must be used so that edges can be 'lost'. Soft pencils, charcoal, chalk and pastels are ideal media. The fading out of tone may be achieved in a number of ways. In figure 102 the shaded areas have been faded out by smudging with a finger. A finger can also be used to offset darker tone from one area and build up light tones in other areas. Similarly, edges of shaded areas can be phased out by soft application of an eraser, and likewise a dirty eraser can be used to rub in tone in other areas. Small pieces of rag and cotton-wool can be used in a similar way. These may be used dry or slightly damp.

102

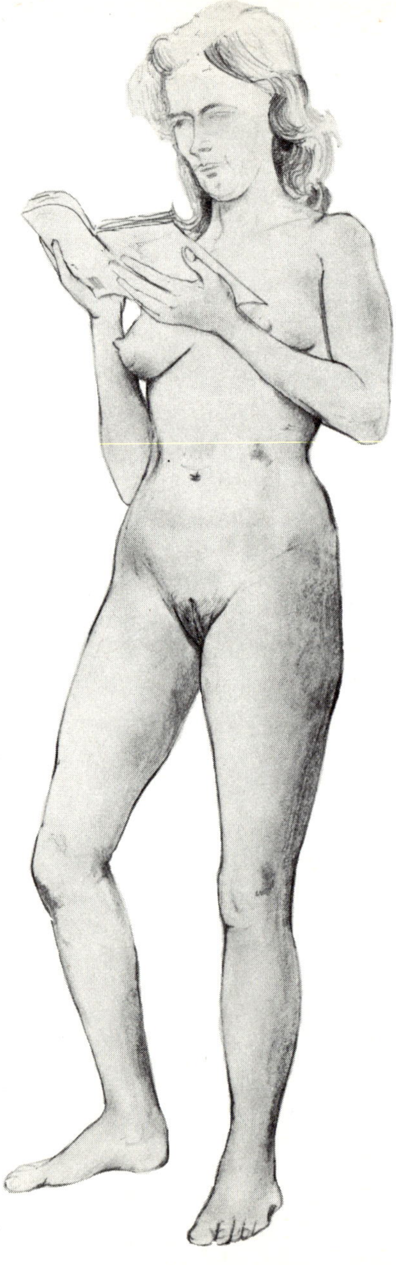

Sir Peter Lely: *A herald*
Black and white chalk on blue-grey toned paper.
Victoria and Albert Museum. Crown copyright

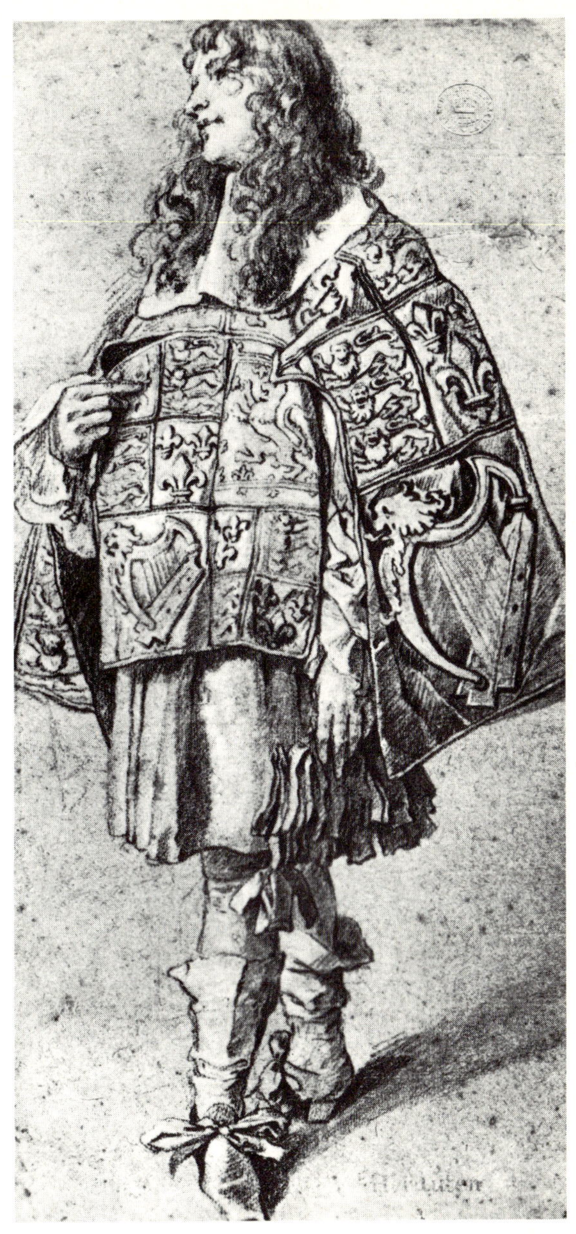

In figure 103 gradations of tone are formed by cross-hatching and smudged with a finger.

In figure 104 the bottle shape was built up by the offsetting and working in of chalk and charcoal into a Conté base.

It should be noted that, as always, the quality and texture of the drawing paper must be considered. Charcoal and chalk, for example, will require the use of heavier paper. Should there be any doubt as to the suitability of a particular type of paper it is advisable to make some simple tests on a scrap of paper of the same type.

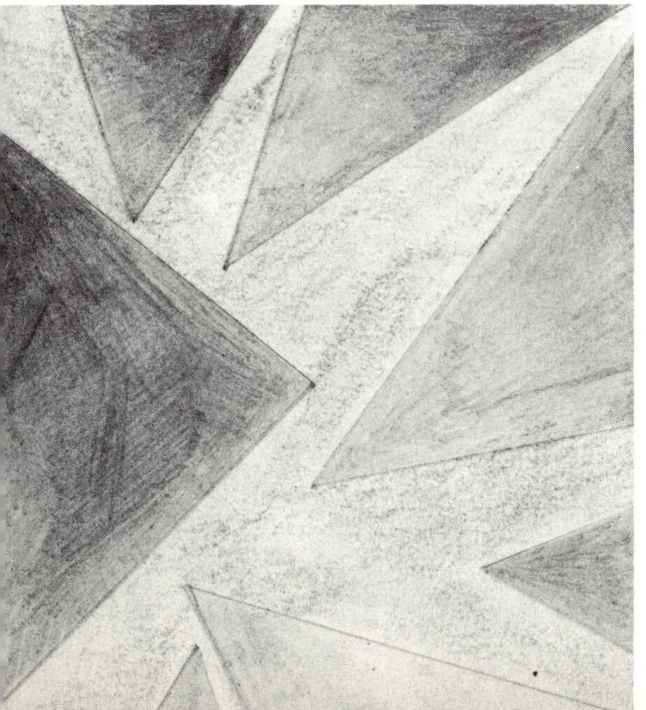

103

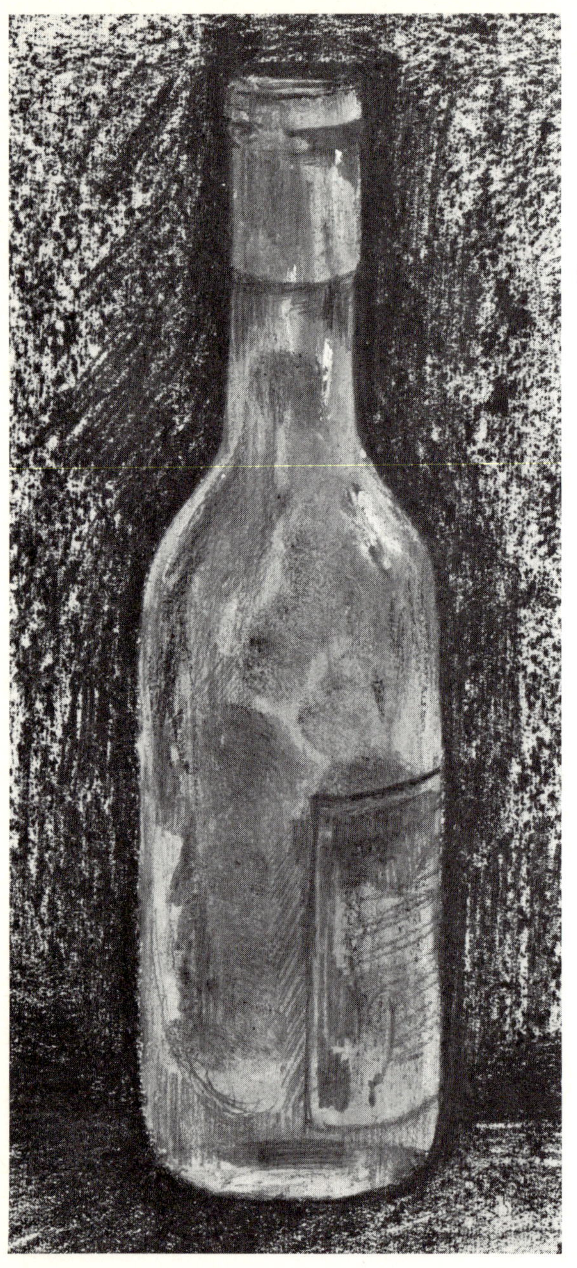

Accumulated tone

104 An alternative way of creating gradations and contrasts in tone is simply by making variations in the build up or deposit of a particular medium. A heavy coating will give dark shadows whilst lighter coatings will create intermediate tones.

It will be necessary to use a soft drawing medium and to select a suitable drawing paper. Techniques for shading, such as cross-hatching, and those for obtaining 'sfumato' effects may be equally well applied here.

Figure 105: accumulated tone with charcoal pencil and Conté.

Figure 106: chalk.

Figure 107: Conté.

105

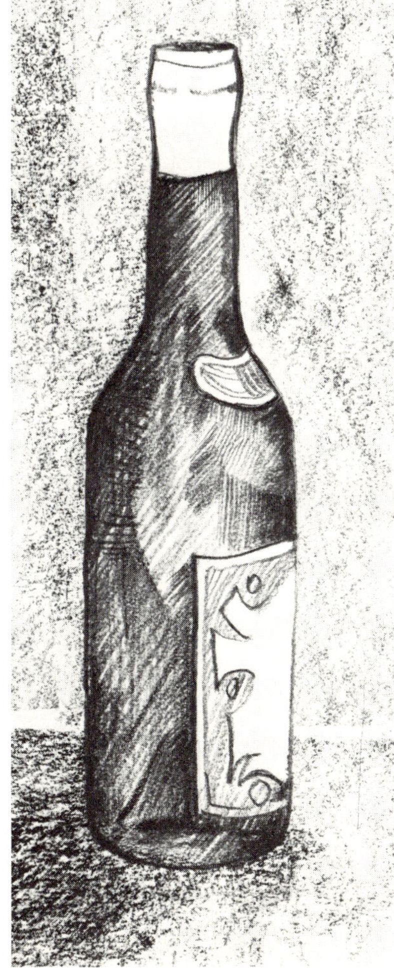

106

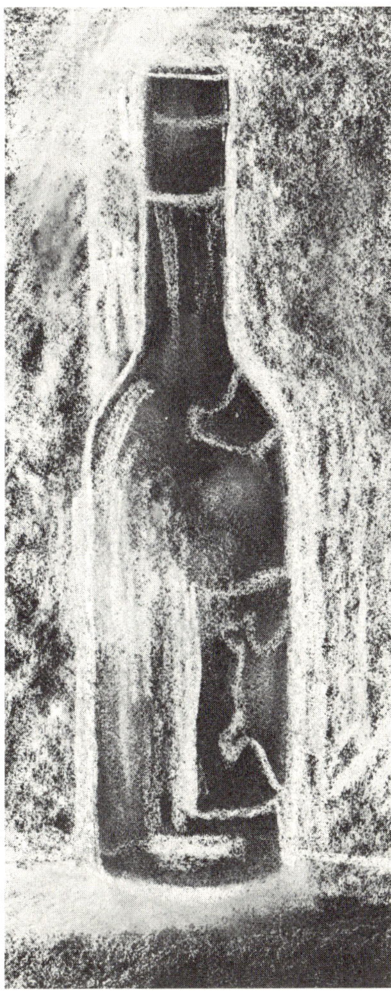

107

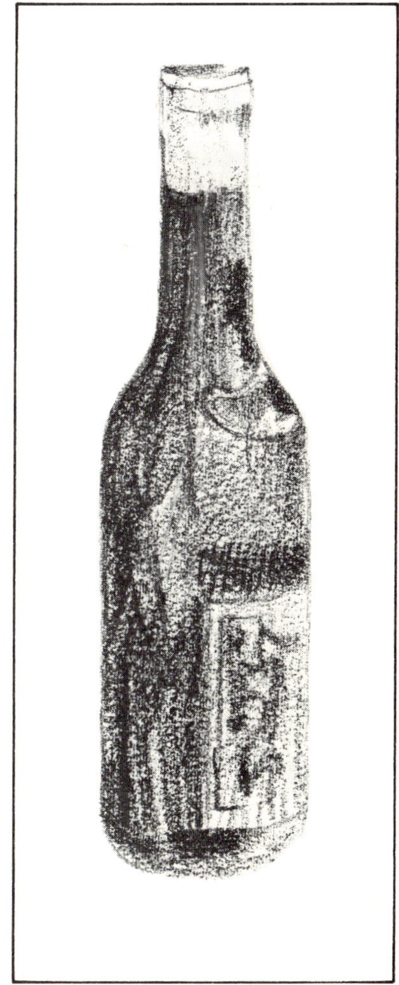

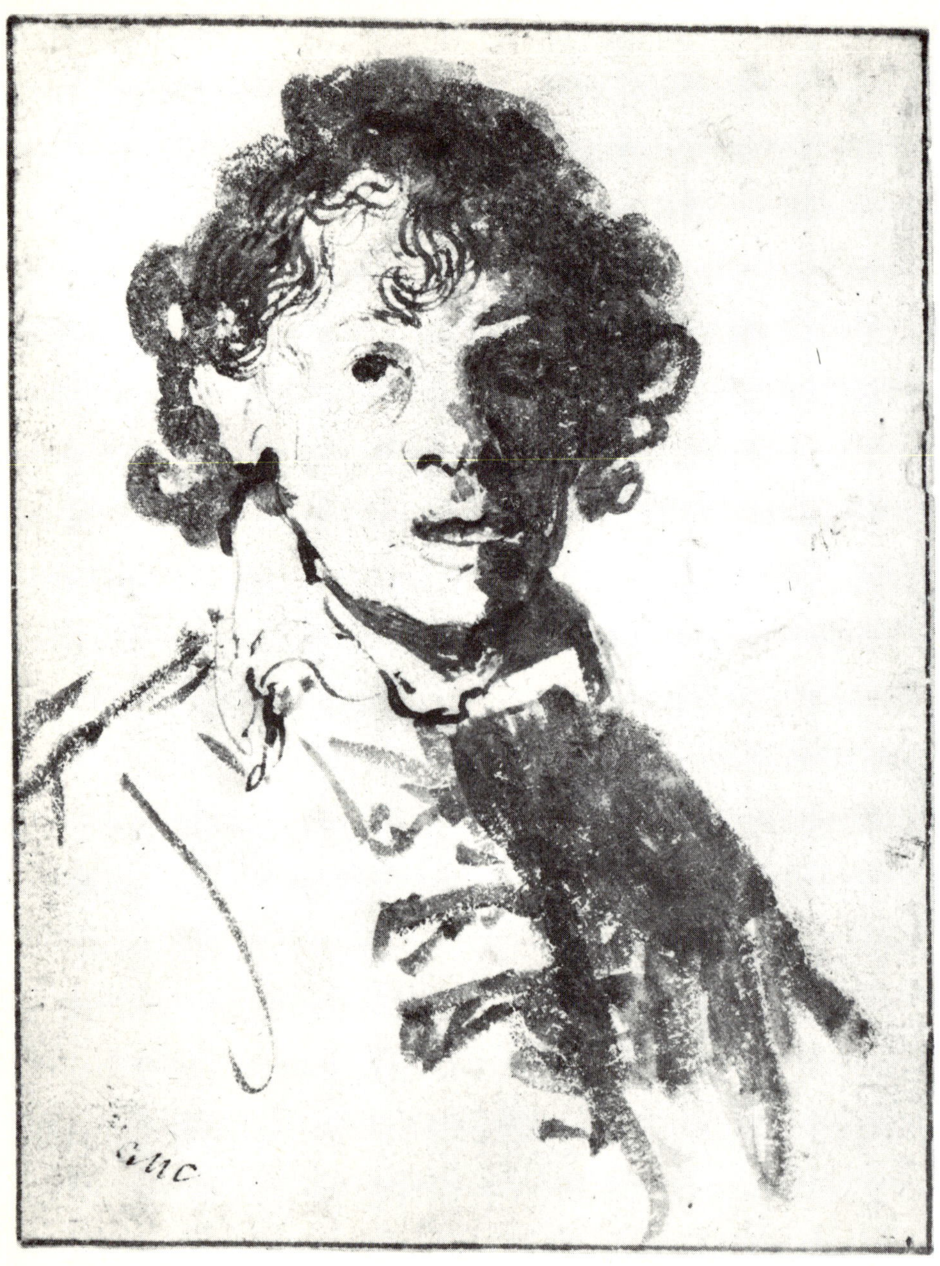

REMBRANDT VAN RIJN:
Self-Portrait (1627–28)
Pen and bistre,
brush and Indian ink
The British Museum

Combining media

The tonal properties of a number of different media can be exploited within an individual drawing. Each medium will have its own natural tone and therefore the medium is selected primarily for this reason. A dark tone, for example, might be obtained with indian ink, whilst a very light tone could be made with charcoal which has been lightly applied and rubbed in.

It is not necessary to use a large variety of drawing tools and media, although splendid abstract drawings can be made in this way, see figure 108. Two or three different media chosen specifically for their suitability for expressing something of the character of the subject can give many different tonal effects. Some media work particularly well together in producing a balanced range of tones; ink, charcoal, charcoal pencil and pencils, for example, in figure 109.

There is not space to illustrate all the many combinations of media possible, but experiments should be made by the individual. The following are suggested as some of the more obvious combinations: charcoal and charcoal pencil; charcoal and chalk; Conté and charcoal pencil; Conté with charcoal pencil plus chalk for highlights; charcoal and ink wash; wash and pen drawing; pencil or charcoal pencil and wash; wax and wash plus pen drawing; wash with felt-tip pen; pencils and charcoal, etc.

Other techniques involving the combined use of

108

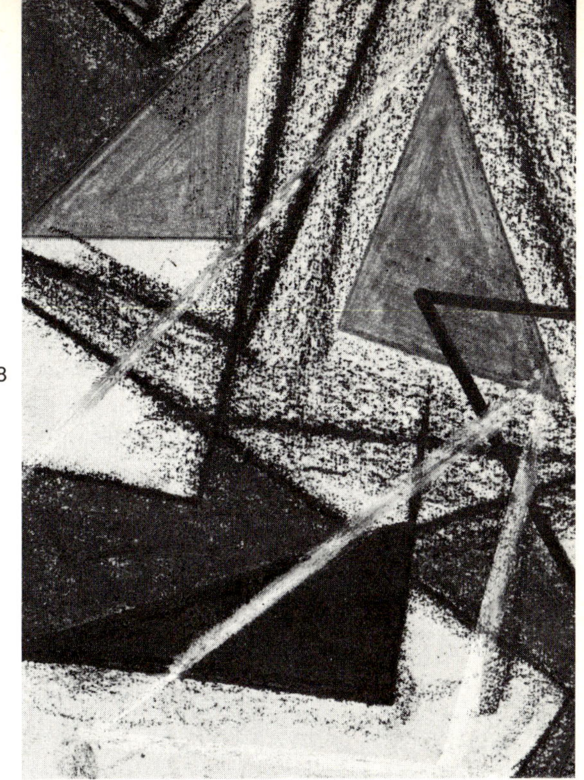

109

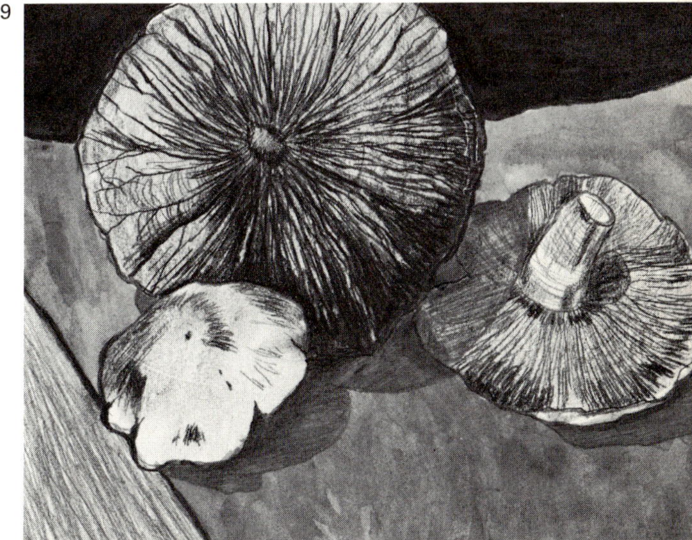

media are described in a later section of this book.

Drawing using resist techniques, textures, stippling and spraying offer exciting possibilities. In figure 110 the sky area was made with ink sprayed on, using a diffuser. If desired, areas to be sprayed can be masked out to protect other parts of the paper from spray drift.

110

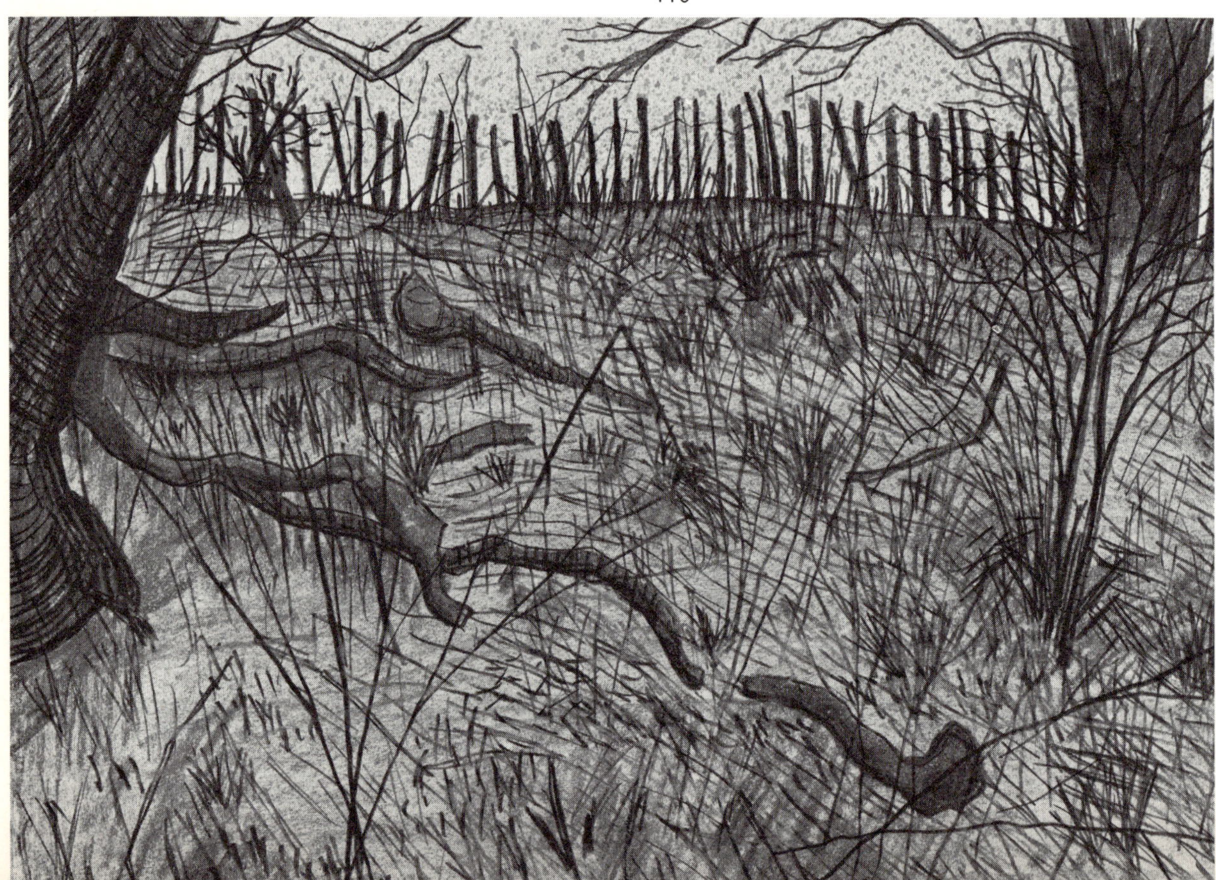

Erasing and heightening

An eraser, as has already been mentioned, is useful for phasing out tone and for softening edges. To create a very soft line, or to lessen the strength of a line gradually, it is often easier to draw it in first quite boldly and then lightly drag an eraser over it. An eraser can also produce very effective highlights or reflections, especially those which occur on glass or shining metal. In this case, a small, clean piece of eraser is used to rub out the relevant parts from an area which was previously covered with some form of tone. The erased parts will then contrast with the shaded areas around them. The highlights in figure 111 were achieved in this way.

In a similar way, chalk may be used to create reflections and highlights in drawings which have been made with charcoal, Conté, or ink. Chalk may also be worked in to areas coated with such media to make lighter areas of tone, see figure 104.

111

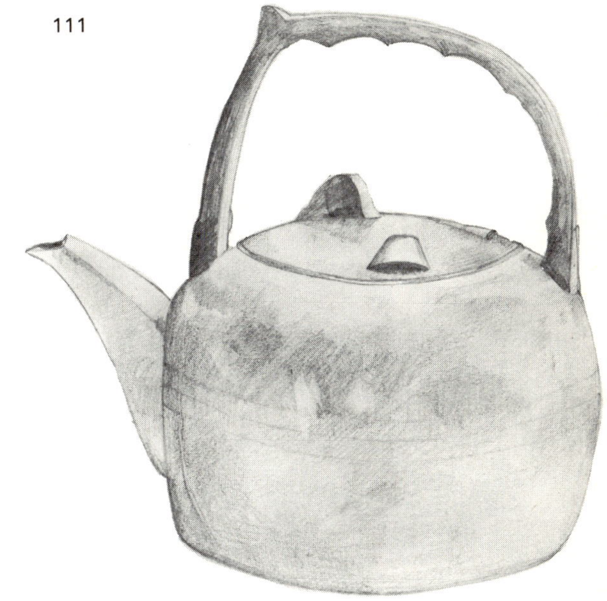

Texture

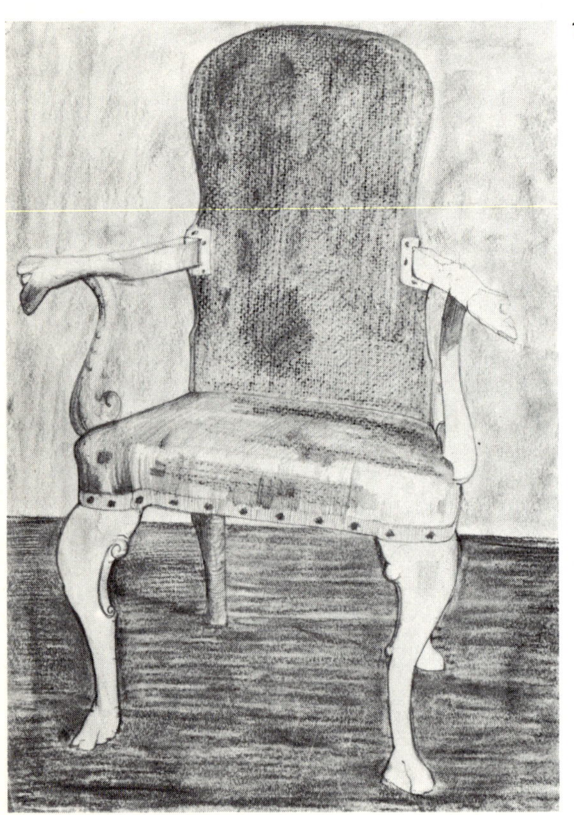

112

The use of texture is dealt with in more detail in a later section but it is relevant here to point out how textures might suitably combine with tone. Some objects will have a heavy textured appearance and in order to convey this in the drawing it may be possible to take a rubbing of a surface of similar character. It will be necessary to draw in the outline of the particular shape first of all, and then to take the rubbing carefully so as to fill in this shape. Areas of tone can then be worked in to the textured parts, which are treated just as any other shaded area.

In figure 112 the chair back suggested this treatment and its textured look was achieved by taking a rubbing from the course side of a small piece of hardboard (fibreboard).

SAMUEL PALMER: *Valley with a Bright Cloud*
Pen and sepia wash. Ashmolean Museum, Oxford

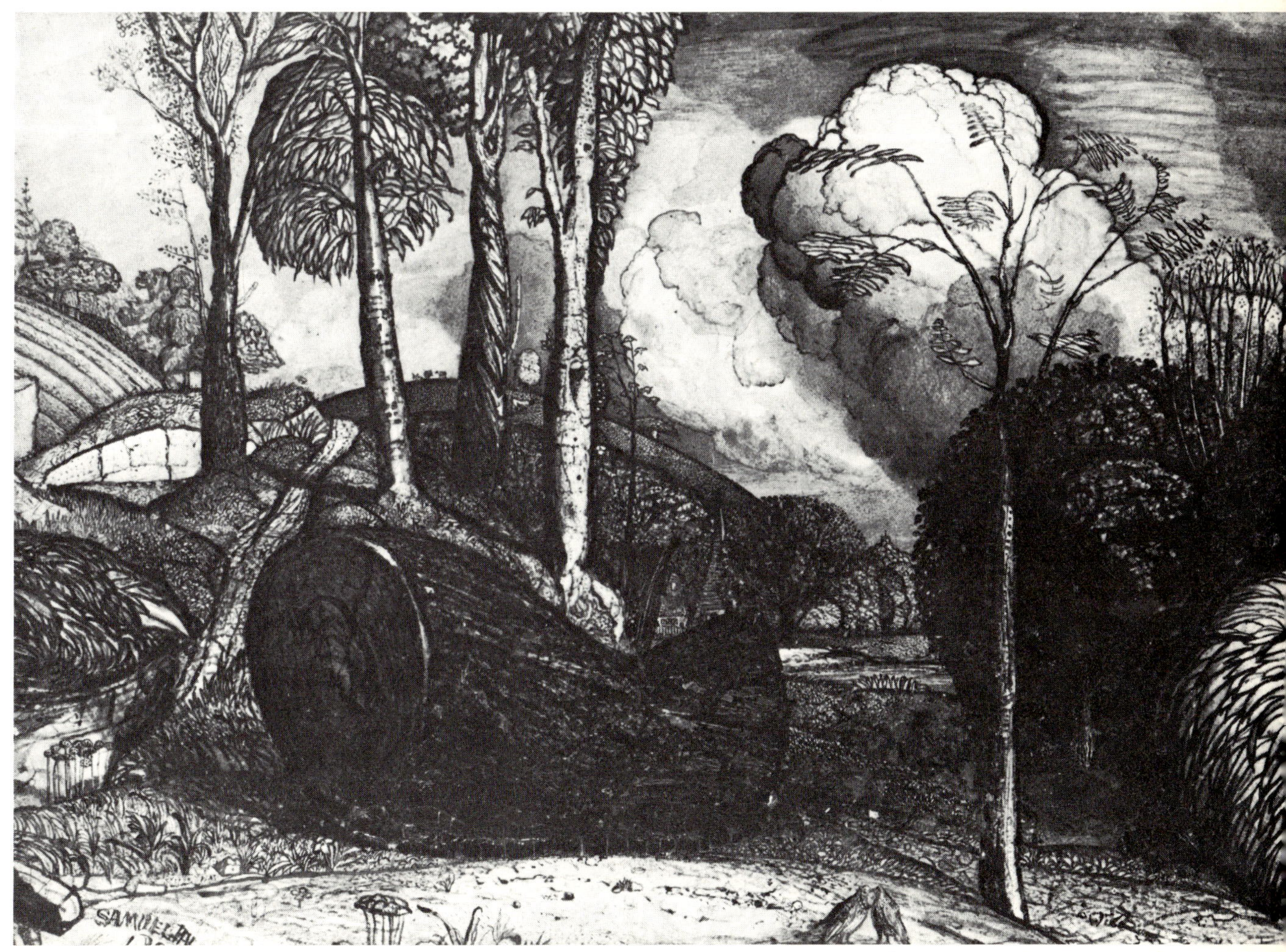

Wash

113

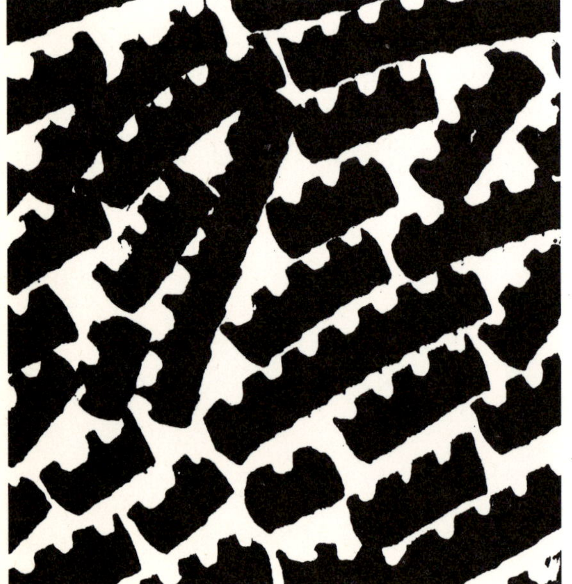

114

Wash drawings are normally made with a brush using different tones of ink or paint. This is an ideal technique to employ for making studies, particularly of landscape, which are later to be worked from for larger compositions in oils or other media.

The traditional way of using wash is to regard the white paper as the highlight, then to apply transparent washes one over another in order to achieve gradations of colour or tone. It is usually necessary to allow each colour or tone to dry before applying the next wash, the gradual accumulation of paint giving variations in the richness of colour and the depth of tones. Alternatively the wash may be applied to individual areas of the drawing as a separate tone with no overpainting. It can be applied to a wet base or against a wet edge and allowed to infuse with it. Whilst a wash is still wet it may be scratched into with the blunt end of a paint brush or similar instrument. When dry, it may be worked over with chalk, charcoal and other media.

Water paints or drawing inks are the most

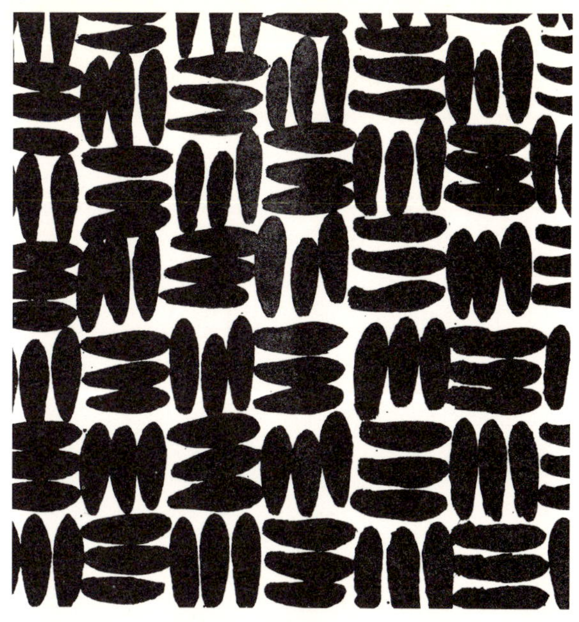

115

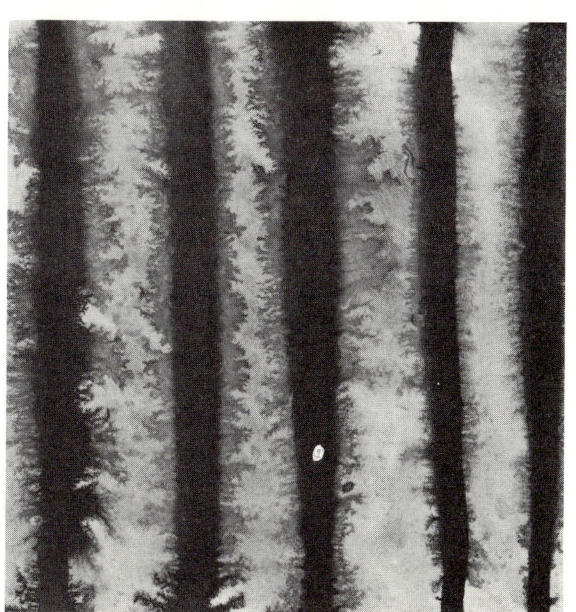

116

suitable media. Indian (drawing) ink is especially good as once it is dry it is permanent and thus successive washes give a glazed effect. Also, it can be diluted with water to produce variations of tone. Brushes of different types and sizes, rags, sponges and tissue paper are useful for applying the wash. Paper of a reasonably absorbent character is required; good quality cartridge (drawing) paper is suitable as well as the heavier papers recommended for work in watercolour.

Paper which receives a lot of wash may wrinkle and thus become difficult to work on as well as presenting problems when mounting or framing. For work other than quick sketches and studies it may therefore be advisable to stretch the paper before use. To do this the paper is first soaked in clean water, either by holding it under the tap or by applying water to it with a large sponge. Strips of gummed paper are then used along the edges of the paper to stick it to a drawing board or similar working surface. When it has dried and the drawing has been completed the paper may be carefully removed and trimmed to the desired size.

Some preliminary exercises with brush and wash will give confidence and stimulate fresh ideas. Different brushes will produce different effects though it is surprising what results are possible with a single brush if used skilfully. Increasing the pressure on a soft brush, for example, will cause it to splay out and give a wider area of wash, as illustrated in figure 113. The brush may be held with both hands and 'rolled' by twisting the handle round and round, giving the effect illustrated in figure 114. A laden, soft brush may be offset, as in figure 115. Figure 116 shows how brush lines splay out into delicate patterns when applied to damp paper, whilst figure 117 is an exercise in making gradations of tone. This was made in indian ink using areas of single tone as well as the accumulative technique.

These methods may be used in drawings to produce contrasts or textural effects, and combined with other methods described on the following pages will give scope for a work of considerable variety.

117

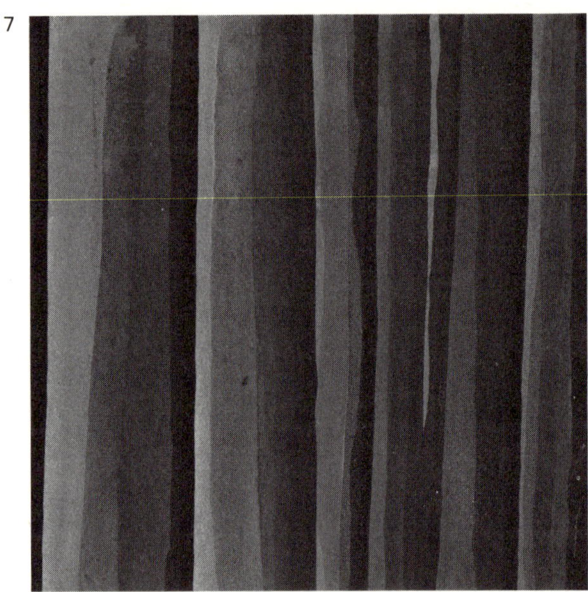

Brush and wash

Wash areas can be contrasted with more detailed brush work. Such drawings may be in a single tone, as in figure 118, or may incorporate gradations of tone and a succession of washes. When dry, areas of wash can be worked over with other media. In figure 119 a fairly dry, stiff-haired brush has been used over the foreground wash area to create the impression of grass. In figure 121 the sky (wash) has been drawn over with chalk and charcoal as well as stippled over with ink.

A variety of brushes can be used, as well as different colours or tones. Extensive, solid areas of wash should be painted in quickly using a large, flat brush.

Resist techniques may also be used. Brush drawing in turpentine, bleach, or liquid wax prior to a wash of paint or ink will give interesting results. Similarly, wash may be applied over drawings made with wax crayons. Figure 120 uses wax resist and spray techniques. See also figure 24.

118

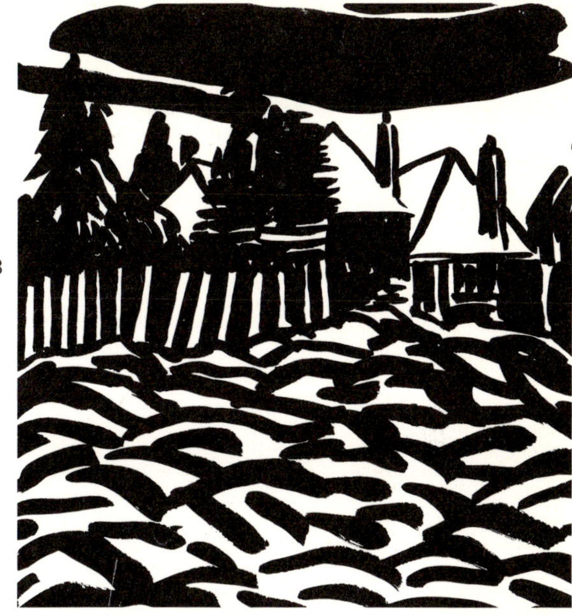

119

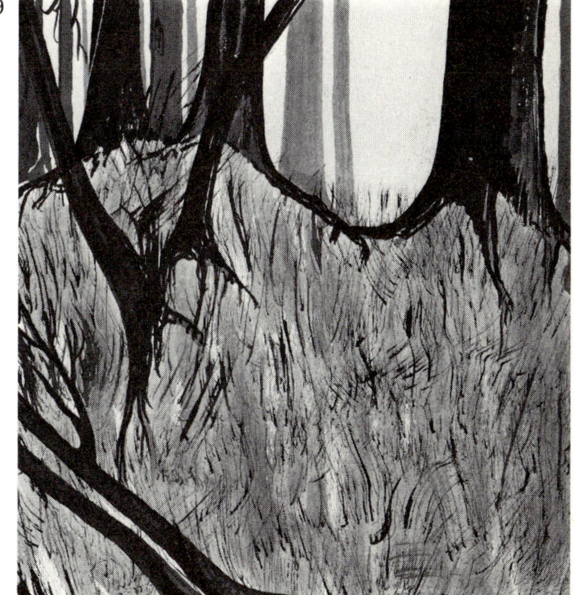

120

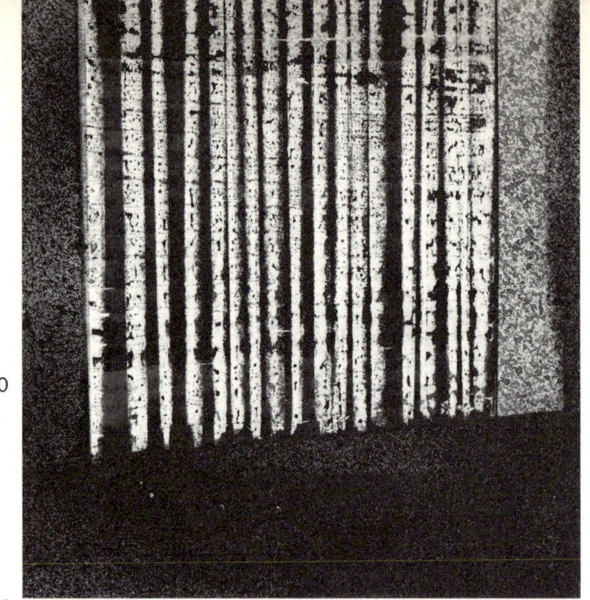

121

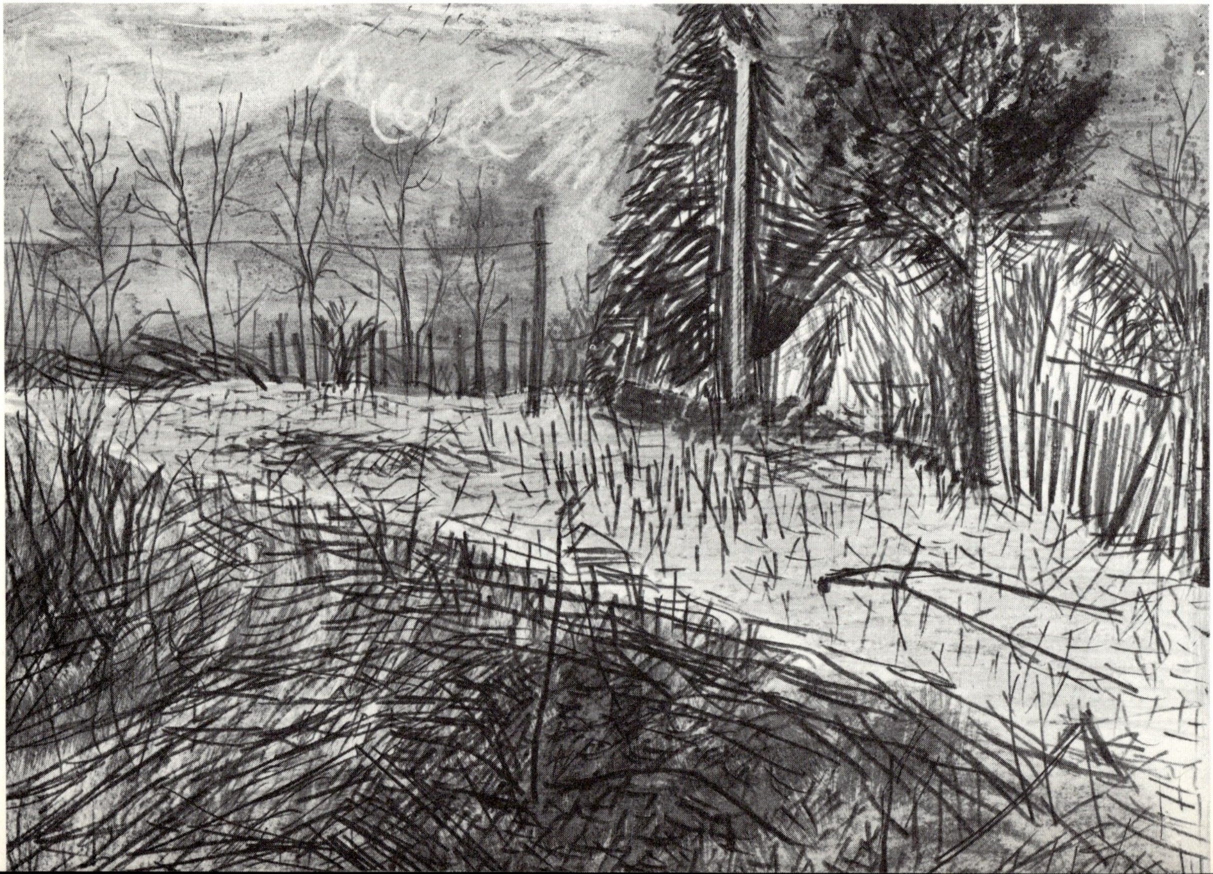

Pen and wash

Pen drawing can also be used for detail work against a background of washes. Different kinds of pens may be used: mapping pens and dip pens with nibs of various widths, fountain pens, special drawing pens, felt-tip pens (fibre-tip) and ball-point pens.

Pen drawing can be used with pencils or other media. It may be confined to purely outline work or can extend over the wash areas, as in figure 122.

122

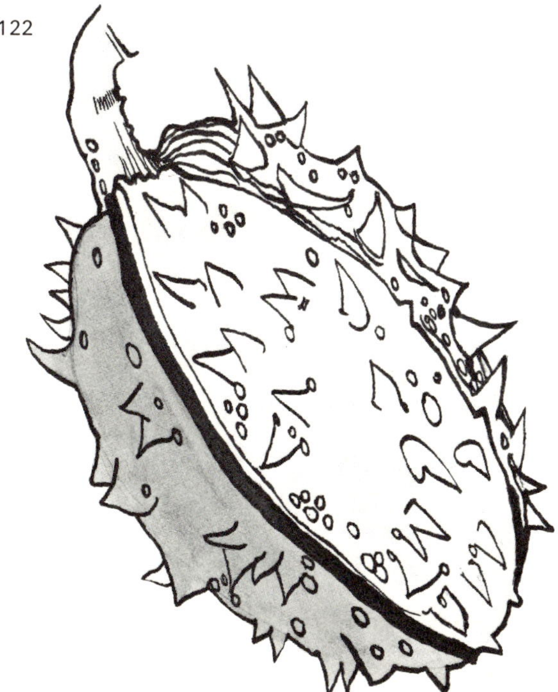

123

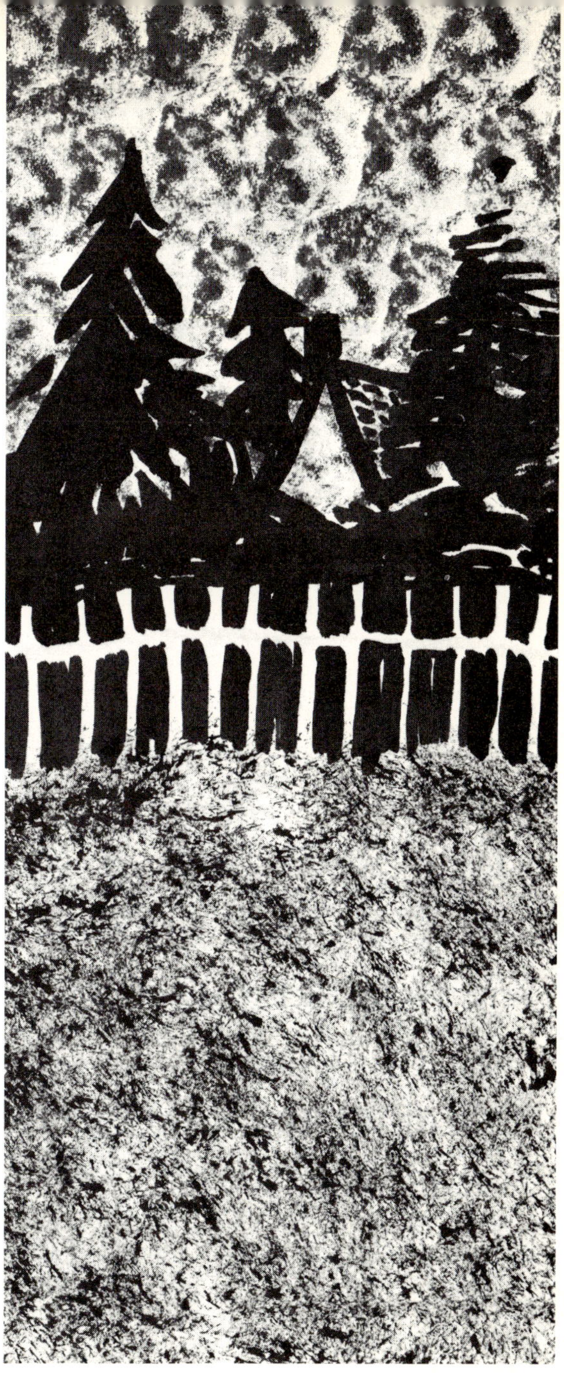

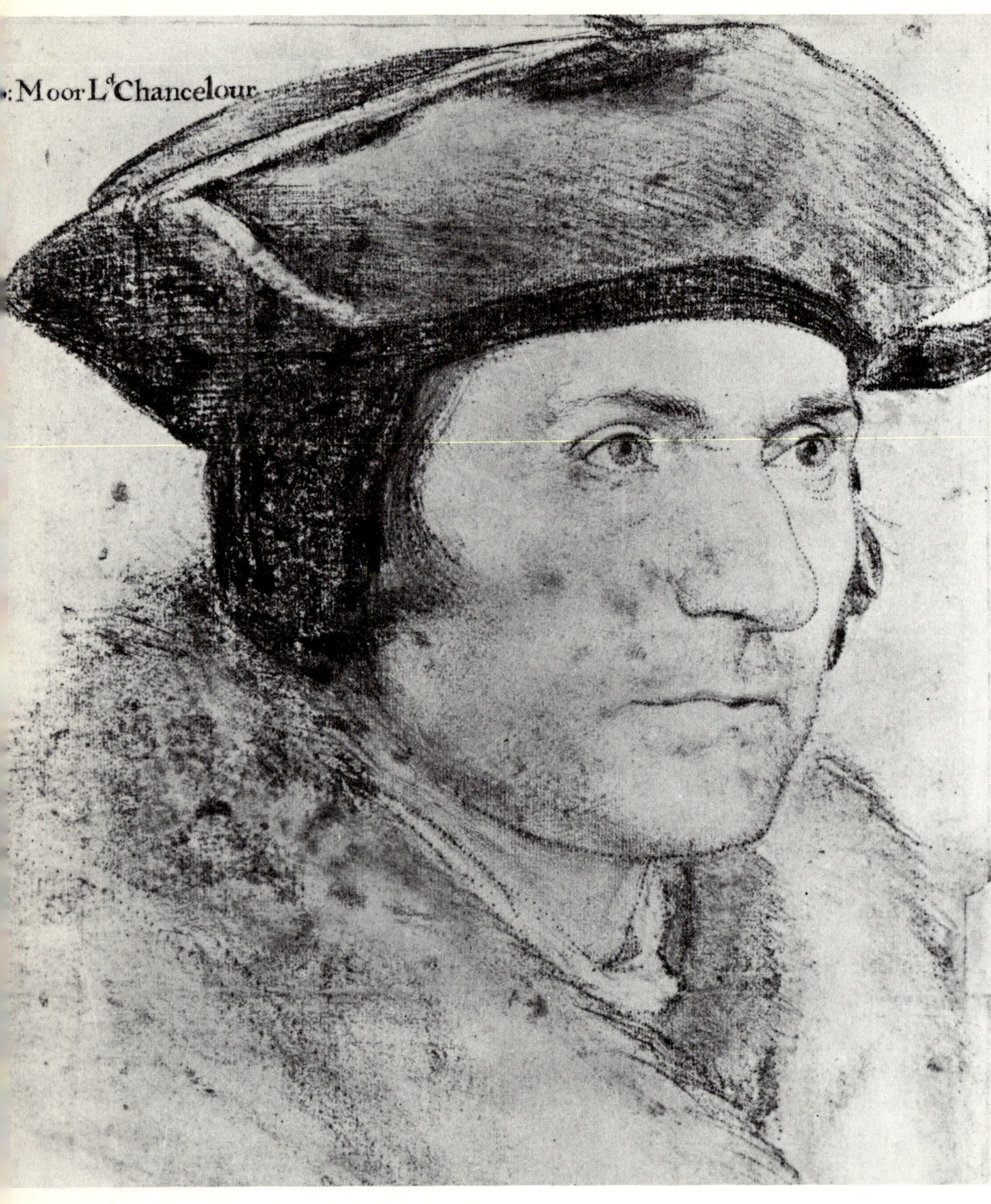

HANS HOLBEIN:
Sir Thomas More
Black and coloured chalk
Reproduced by gracious permission of Her Majesty the Queen

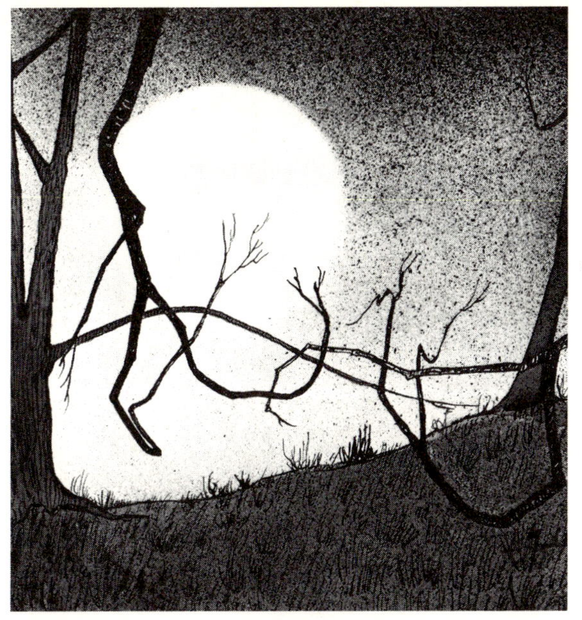

124

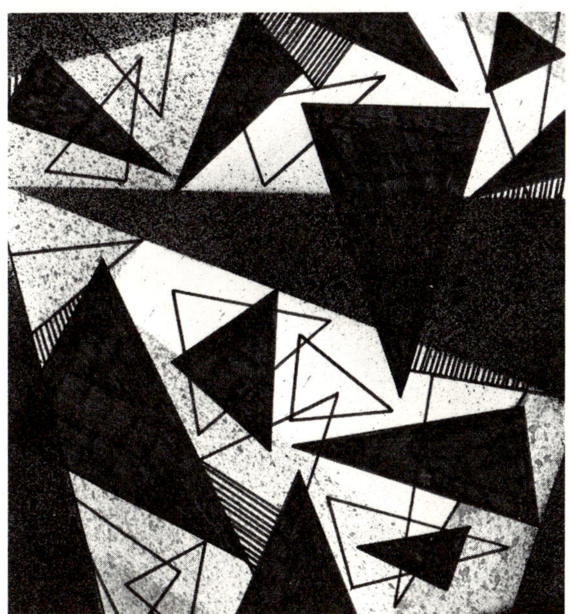

125

Other wash techniques

Wash may be applied in a number of other ways. Sponges of various sizes and textures are useful for laying in large areas of wash and for stippling. Wash can also be applied with tissue paper or small pieces of rag. These may be used to dab on paint or ink, as in figure 123 (the sky), or perhaps to wipe them on lightly. Tints of colour can be applied by using coloured tissue paper which has been dipped in clean water.

Areas of broken tone can be stippled or sprayed in. A quite large, stiff-haired brush is best for stippling; it should be used fairly dry. Spray is applied from an aerosol can or by using a spray diffuser. Sprayed and stippled areas are normally executed before other drawing. If required, areas can be masked out with newspaper or scrap paper so that they are left free of sprayed or stippled paint; templates can be cut to desired shapes and sizes. To avoid smudging, the paint or ink should be allowed to dry before templates or paper masks are removed.

The foreground of figure 123 shows the use of stippled ink, whilst figures 124 and 125 involve the use of sprayed areas.

Texture

In this context, texture means an interesting division of the surface area; with drawing techniques it is seldom possible to achieve impasto effects and thus a drawing cannot have the same tactile qualities that might be found in a painting, or on a piece of pottery, or a length of woven fabric. This is a surface division that appeals to the vision rather than the touch. Textured shapes can be used as interesting contrasts to other methods of drawing; they can relate directly to the character of the object being drawn, see figure 112.

A drawing in which texture is involved needs some preliminary thought and planning. It is not always possible to isolate a particular shape of texture and therefore it may be necessary to apply a general texture which is later worked over. Alternatively, parts may have to be masked out before texturing. The surface might have to be prepared in some other way: the texture might, for example, be applied over an area of light wash. The methods of working will depend on various factors and must be planned in relation to individual drawings.

126

Rubbings

There are many interesting surfaces around us, in the home, at school, or in nature, and textures may be obtained from these in the form of rubbings. Such textures may be confined to certain shapes within the drawing, they may take the form of a general ground, or they may be superimposed on areas of wash, pencil or other media.

Heelball, wax crayons, Conté or chalk are the most useful for taking rubbings. Cartridge (drawing) paper is generally suitable, but thinner quality paper such as newsprint can be used if the texture is shallow or elaborate. When selecting the paper one must also consider its suitability for other types of drawing if the rubbing is to be combined with other techniques. Coloured paper can be used or coloured crayons on white paper. Rubbings can be combined or superimposed in different tones, the texture forming a design in its own right, see figure 127.

When taking a rubbing the paper is placed over the textured surface and held firmly in place whilst the crayon is rubbed systematically across it. The crayon is used on its side and it is usually best to rub it across in one direction and then in the opposite direction, applying pressure gradually. With deep textures care must be taken not to tear the paper.

In figure 128 the rubbing forms the background for an offset design. Rubbings may also be taken from card templates. See also figures 51 and 112.

127

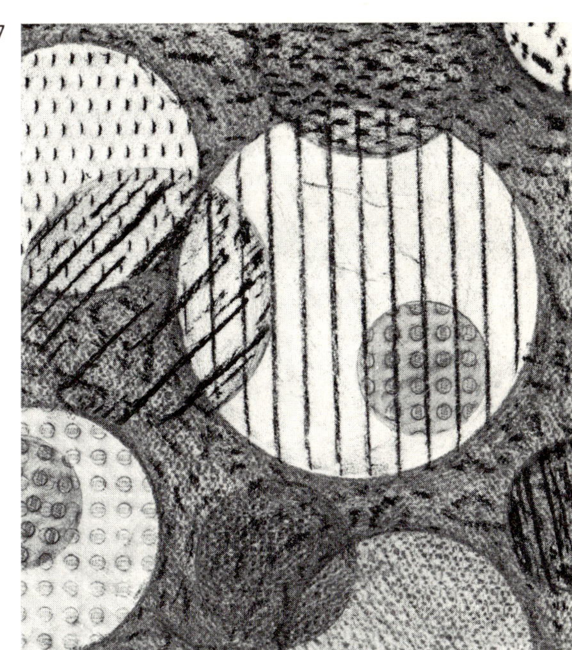

Offset texture

Small, screwed up pieces of paper or cloth which have been dipped in ink or paint may be pressed down in parts of a drawing to form an offset texture, see figure 126. Engraved sticks and potatoes as well as small shapes of textured material may be used in a similar way. General tones can be applied by offsetting charcoal or Conté, see page 64.

A fairly dry stiff-haired brush lightly dragged across the paper will also give an interesting texture and the same principle applied to roller and ink.

In figure 128 a spray of leaves was coated with ink before being offset on to a textured ground.

128

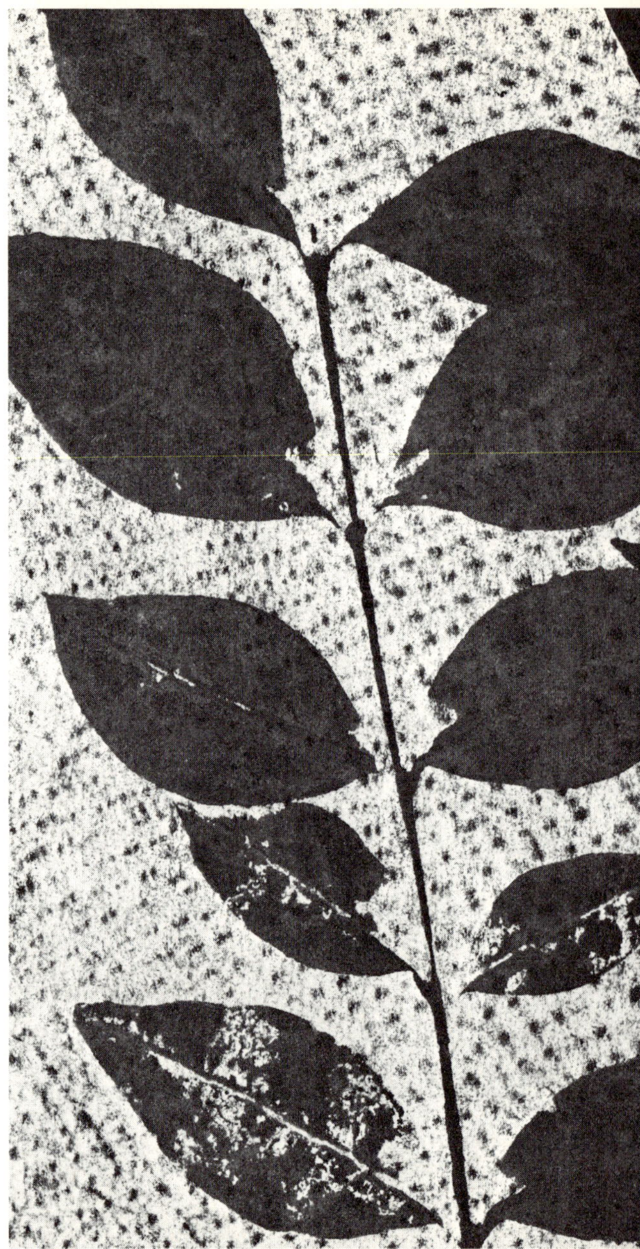

Stippled and sprayed texture

Texture applied by stippling may easily be confined to certain parts of a drawing. Stippling is done with a stiff-haired brush used in a fairly dry state. Interesting grounds are obtained by spraying. Ink and paint can be sprayed on with a spray diffuser, or aerosol cans used. Paint normally has to be thinned and, as in figure 129, it may be necessary to mask out shapes prior to spraying.

129

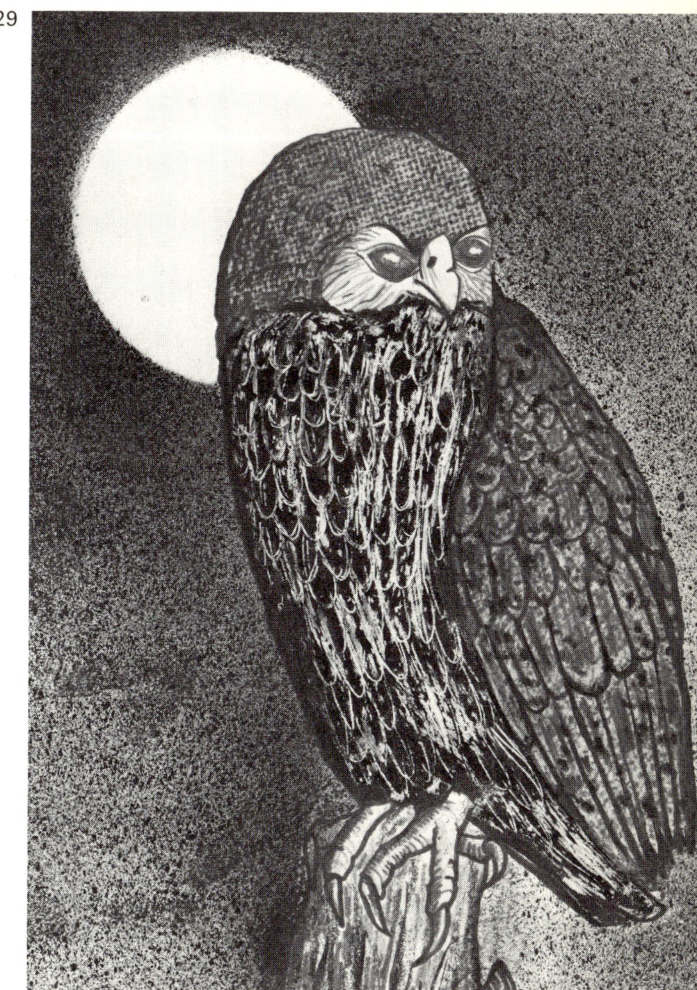

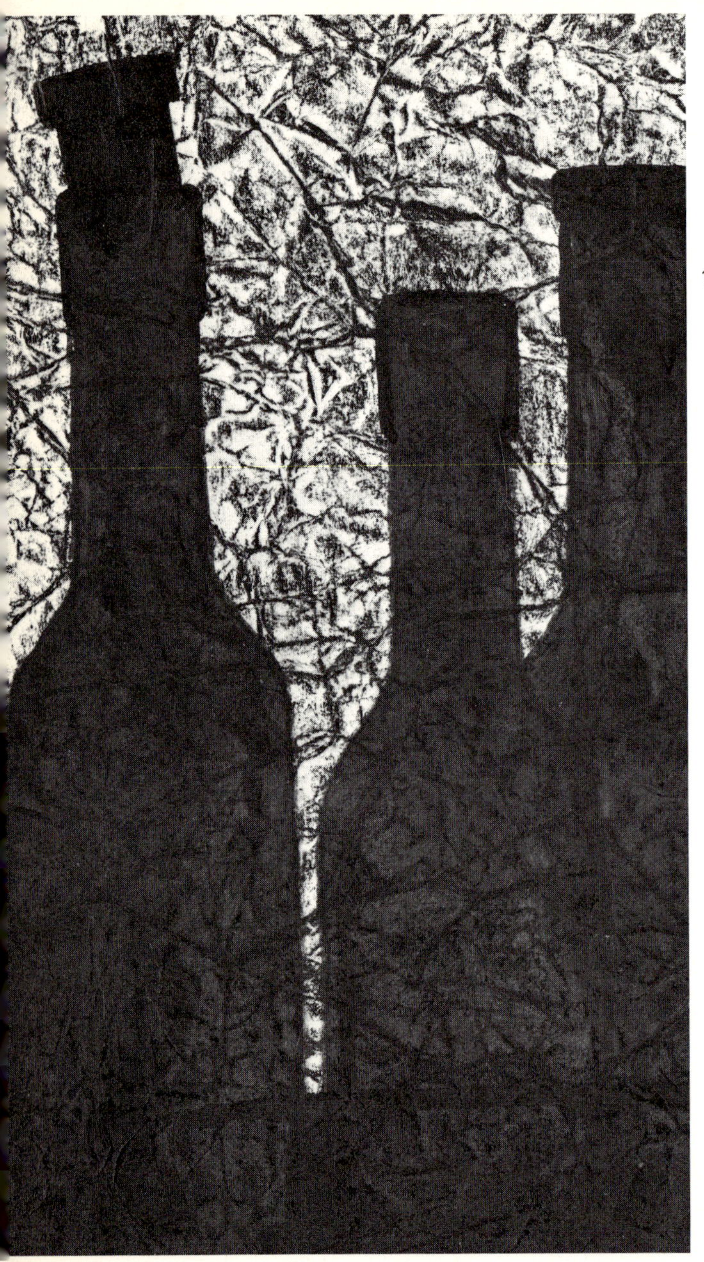

Impasto and other methods

130 Texture can be built up by combining techniques and media, for example, ink stippled over a wax rubbing. Impasto qualities can only be achieved in a relative sense; thick paint can be used for brush drawings, and ink can be used with powdered chalk.

Other methods might make use of heavily textured paper or paper which has been crinkled. Paper which has been screwed up and then flattened out may be given a coating of wax crayon, chalk, charcoal or Conté with the result illustrated in figure 130. Resist techniques also give interesting textures: ink or paint over wax or turpentine for example. Textured grounds may be prepared by sprinkling sand over glued paper.

Other ideas and techniques

Other ideas can combine different media, or may involve some special preparation of the paper before drawing.

Mosaic drawings

Mosaic drawings must be done on small sheets of paper or card; their total effect depends upon neat, accurate work. The drawings may be executed in pencil or in a combination of media. The paper is first divided up into squares. Lines or shapes are then drawn over the squares so that they are dissected in various ways. By using this method of working the design may be shaped more easily. Alternatively, the lines and shapes may be drawn first and these subsequently divided by squaring up; the advantage here being that the design can be erased and altered more easily. Areas are then shaded in so that they are bordered by an area of a different colour and medium. Where a square is subdivided, each part is treated individually.

Figure 131 shows a pencil mosaic drawing. Note that the 'rule' for filling in alternate shapes cannot always apply when only one medium is used.

Figure 132 is a variation. A continuous line has been subdivided into shapes by arcs; two media have been used.

Again, numerous alternatives are possible.

131

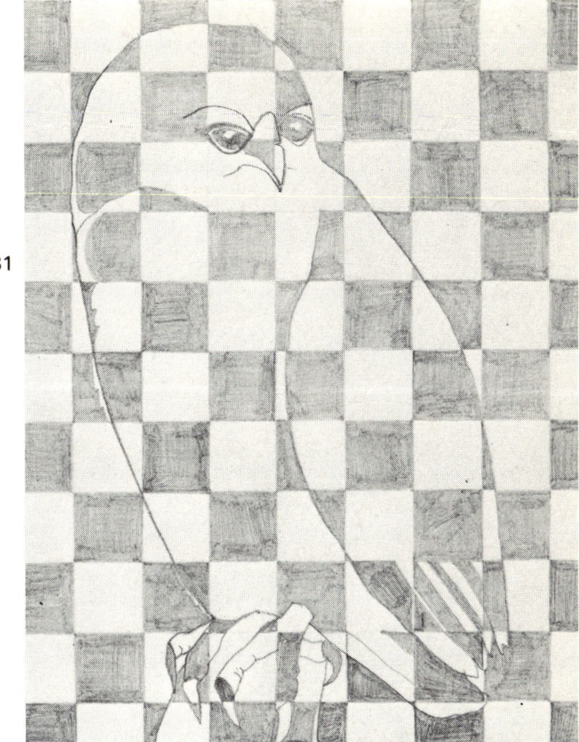

132

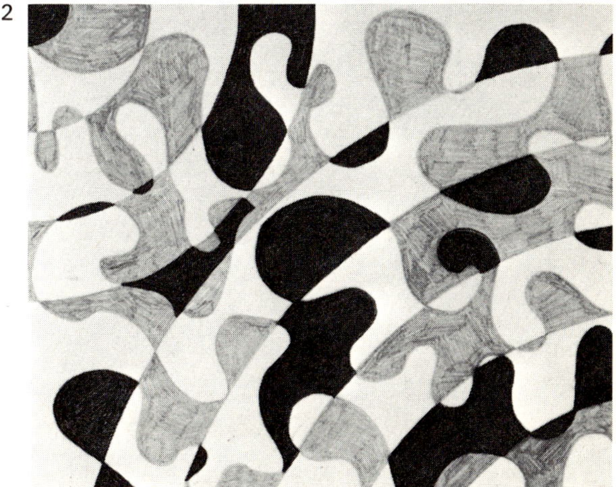

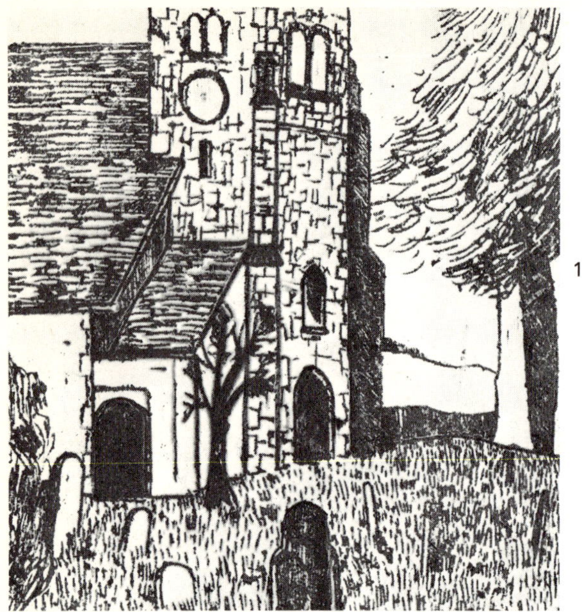

133

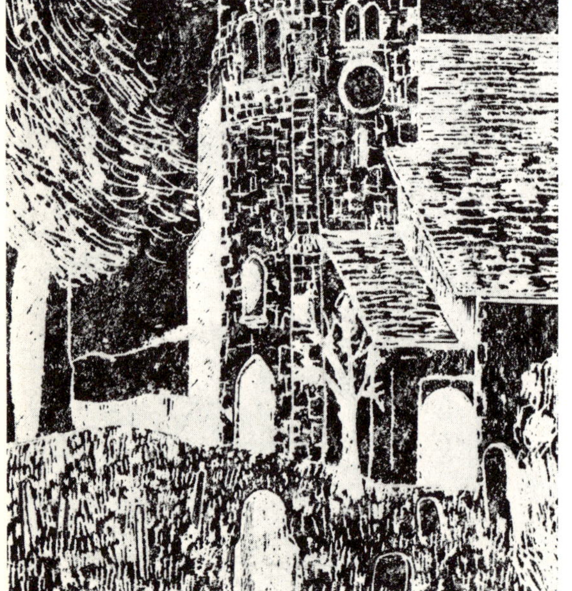

134

Chalk and wax

Interesting positive/negative drawings can be made using chalk and wax. The paper is folded in half. The right-hand half is coated first with a layer of white chalk, then with one of wax. It is important that the chalk covers all parts of the paper and that no gaps are left, similarly with the wax. A coloured wax crayon may be used. The paper is then folded over and a design drawn, pressing down on to the wax coating underneath. Any drawing instrument which will give a firm impression may be used; pencils and ball-point pens are usually the most suitable. When the paper is opened out the drawn parts will have offset on to the left-hand side of the fold with a positive/negative result. See figures 133 and 134.

Chalk and charcoal may be used in exactly the same way.

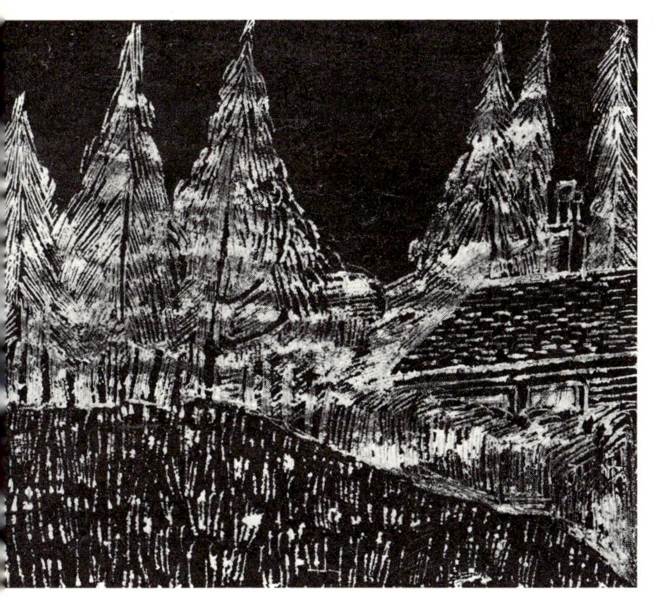

135

Wax etching

Wax etchings are made by first coating the paper with small, thick areas of wax crayon. Black should not be used. The whole paper is then covered with indian ink until none of the wax shows. When this has dried, lines and areas can be scratched away with a fine point or knife, revealing the wax colours beneath.

In figure 135 white wax was used resulting in a drawing similar in character to scraperboard.

A similar effect, though not so predictable, may be achieved by using ink over chalk.

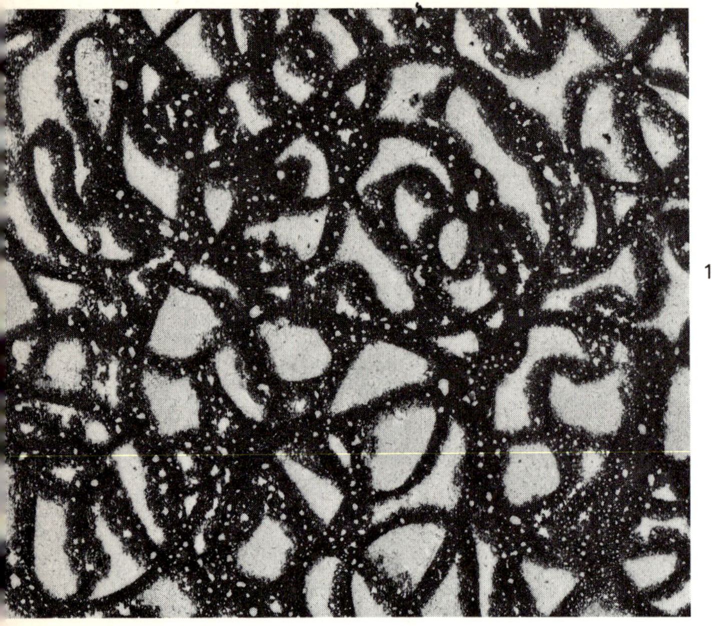

136

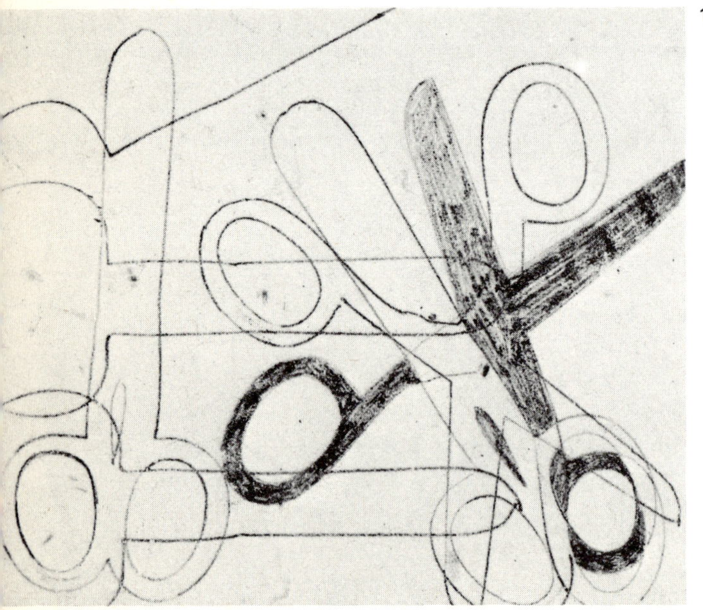

137

Resist drawings

Various resist techniques have already been mentioned, see figures 23, 24, 120.

Figure 136 is a scribble drawing in black wax crayon on black paper. When the drawing was finished the paper was washed over with white water-colour.

Paper which has been coated with wax crayon may be used in a similar way to carbon paper, and copies of original drawings or designs may be obtained in this way, see figure 137.

Once again variations are possible and different media may be exploited.

Technical notes

Tools and media

Experiments should be made with a large variety of drawing tools and media. Each medium will have its own characteristics and limitations; experience with a particular medium is necessary to explore its potentiality. Drawings can be made with the following: pencils of various types, including carpenters' pencils, charcoal pencils and coloured pencils; charcoal; Conté; pastels; wax-crayons; chalks; oil pastels; inks and paints; felt-tip and fibre-tip pens; ball-point pens; dip-pens; stylographs; fountain pens; and brushes. Drawings can also be made by erasing, cutting with scissors, scratching or engraving with a knife, nail or sharp point, as well as offset with a comb, sponge, piece of rag, and so on. Further suggestions are made in the text and others can be invented.

Papers

The paper must be selected with regard to the media and techniques to be used. Cartridge (drawing) paper will suit most types of work. This should be of a good quality; 60 lb cartridge paper is recommended.

Sugar paper, newsprint, art paper, card, cardboard and even brown wrapping paper are among other suitable supports; coloured and textured papers are also useful.

Preparation

The paper or support may need preparing in some way before drawing. Paper which is to be subjected to large areas of wash, for example, may need stretching. This is explained on page 75. Card can be sized. Other drawings may require initial applications of wax, spray, texture, etc, as described in the text. The paper should be large enough to allow a margin for mounting or framing.

Reversing

Drawings can be reversed by using tracing paper, by holding them against a window or by using carbon or waxed paper, see page 90. Most printmaking techniques will automatically reverse the original design.

Squaring-up

If a drawing is to be used as preparatory material for a larger study or painting it may be squared-up so that the design within a particular square can be transferred accurately to the corresponding larger square on the canvas, board or paper. The proportions of the larger surface must relate to those of the original drawing. This can be checked by placing the drawing in the top left-hand corner of the larger surface: the diagonal from top left to bottom right of the drawing should then correspond to the same diagonal of the larger area.

Fixing

Most drawing inks are permanent and oil pastels and certain types of crayons do not smudge. Most other media, especially if used in heavy coatings, will need fixing. Fixative is obtainable in aerosol cans or can be applied from a bottle with a spray diffuser. It is a type of thin varnish and prevents drawings offsetting and smudging.

Display

Completed drawings which have been fixed or varnished can be trimmed, mounted and framed. Mounts are best made from thick card of a neutral colour. The drawing is attached to the back of the mount with adhesive tape or glue. Mounts can be framed under glass.

Further reading

The following books are recommended for reading, inspiration and reference:

History and appreciation

Modern Graphics, Keith Murgatroyd, Studio Vista, London; Dutton, New York
Modern Prints and Drawings, Paul Sachs, Knopf, New York
Graphic Art of the 20th Century, Raymond Cogniat, Thames and Hudson, London
1000 Years of Drawing, Anthony Bartram, Studio Vista, London, (out of print)
Drawing/The Appreciation of the Arts 3, Philip Rawson, Oxford University Press, London and New York
The Master Draughtsman series, Zwemmer, London; Borden, California
The Great Draughtsman series, Pall Mall Press, London

Reference, technical and didactic

Bridgeman's Complete Guide to Drawing from Life, Sterling Publishing Co Inc, New York
Grammar of Drawing, Colin Hayes, Studio Vista, London; Van Nostrand Reinhold, New York
Techniques of Drawing, Fred Gettings, Studio Vista, London, (out of print)
Object Drawing Techniques, Calvin Burnett, Van Nostrand Reinhold, New York
Studio Drawing Books, a series edited by Peter Probyn, Studio Vista, London; Watson-Guptill, New York
Preparation for Painting, Lynton Lamb, Penguin Books, Harmondsworth
Drawing Lessons from the Great Masters, Robert Beverly Hale, Studio Vista, London; Watson-Guptill, New York

Ideas and techniques

Pictures with Crayons, Lothar Kampmann, Batsford, London; Watson-Guptill, New York
Pictures with Inks, Lothar Kampmann, Batsford, London; Watson-Guptill, New York
Creative Drawing – Point and Line, Ernst Röttger and Dieter Klante, Batsford, London; Van Nostrand Reinhold, New York
Creative Rubbings, Laye Andrew, Batsford, London; Watson-Guptill, New York
Surfaces in Creative Design, Ernst Röttger, Dieter Klante and Friedrich Salzmann, Batsford, London; Van Nostrand Reinhold, New York
Introducing Graphic Techniques, Robin Capon, Batsford, London
Introducing Graphic Design, Robin Capon, Watson-Guptill, New York
Techniques of Drawing, Howard Simon, Sterling Publishing Co Inc, New York
The Quickest Way to Draw Well, Frederic Taubes, Pitman, London
Elements of Sketching, Geoffrey Fletcher, Allen & Unwin, London

Suppliers

Most drawing equipment is obtainable from local art shops and stationers.

Great Britain

Paints, crayons, inks, paper and all art materials

Fred Aldous, The Handicrafts Centre, 37 Lever Street, Manchester M60 1UX
E. J. Arnold (School Suppliers), Butterley Street, Leeds LS10 1AX
Arts and Crafts, 10 Byram Street, Huddersfield HD1 1DA
Crafts Unlimited, Macklin Street, London WC2
Dryad Limited, Northgates, Leicester
Educational Supply Association, Pinacles, Harlow, Essex
Margros Limited, Monument Way West, Woking, Surrey
Clifford Milburn Limited, 54 Fleet Street, London EC4
Nottingham Handicrafts Company (School Suppliers), Melton Road, West Bridgford, Nottingham (not paints, inks or crayons)
Reeves and Sons Limited, Lincoln Road, Enfield, Middlesex and branches
George Rowney and Company Limited, 10 Percy Street, London W1
Winsor and Newton Limited, 51 Rathbone Place, London W1 and branches

Crayons may be ordered from:
Cosmic Crayon Company, Ampthill Road, Bedford
Harbutt's Limited, Barthampton, Bath, Somerset
Scholarship Industries Limited, Manor Lane, Holmes Chapel, Cheshire

Felt-tip pens
Mentmore Manufacturing Company Limited, Six Hills Way, Stevenage, Herts
Speedry Products Limited, Copers Cope Road, Beckenham, Kent

Paper
Barcham Green Limited, Hayle Mill, Tovil, Maidstone, Kent

Grosvenor Chater and Company Limited, 68 Cannon Street, London EC4
T. N. Lawrence, Bleeding Heart Yard, Greville Street, London EC1
Spicer Cowan Limited, 19 New Bridge Street, London EC4
Strong Hanbury Company Limited, Peterborough Road, Fulham, London SW7

USA

General art materials

Arthur Brown and Bro Inc, 2 West 46 Street, New York
A. I. Friedman Inc, 25 West 45 Street, New York
Grumbacher, 460 West 34 Street, New York
The Morilla Company Inc, 43 21st Street, Long Island City, New York and 2866 West 7 Street, Los Angeles, California
New Masters Art Division: California Products Corporation, 169 Waverley Street, Cambridge, Massachusetts
Stafford-Reeves Inc, 626 Greenwich Street, New York, NY 10014
Steig Products, PO Box 19, Lakewood, New Jersey 08701
Winsor and Newton Inc, 555 Winsor Drive, Secaucus, New Jersey 07094

Felt-tip pens

Magic Marker Corporation, 88 and 73 Avenue Glendale, New York
Nobema Products Corporation, 91 Broadway, Jersey City, New Jersey
The F. Weber Co, Wayne and Windrim Streets, Philadelphia, Pennsylvania

Paper

Chicago Cardboard Co, 1240 N. Homan Avenue, Chicago 51
Hobart Paper Co, 11 West Washington Street, Chicago, Illinois 60600
Japan Paper Co, 100 East 31st Street, New York 16
Wellman Paper Co, 308 West Broadway, New York, NY 10012
Andrew/Nelson/Whitehead Paper Corporation, 7 Laight Street, New York 13